Glory to His Name

Readings for Advent

2024

CHRISSIE SMITH

Glory to His Name: Readings for Advent 2024

Copyright © 2024 by 12 Oaks Press, LLC

To contact the author: chrissieosmith@gmail.com.

Not to us, Lord, not to us
But to Your name give glory
Because of Your mercy
Because of Your truth.

Introduction

Advent—what a beautiful time of year. It's something I look forward to every year. As winter starts to take hold of the earth, the earth starts to slow down. It's a reminder that we, too, need to slow down. Advent is our opportunity to intentionally do just that. But though we may slow down on the outside, on the inside, we're doing a great work. We are preparing our hearts for the Savior.

When we take time during this season of the year to meditate on His coming to earth as a baby, we are also reminded again and again that He will come again—this time as a conquering King. The time to make ourselves ready is now.

Advent observances look different for everyone. Some homes and churches utilize a wreath with four candles which are lit in order each week. Some families schedule special outings and special ministry events that provide the opportunity to share the good news of Jesus with others or to help others who are less fortunate.

However you choose to observe it, Advent should be about transformation, growing closer to Jesus, and moving deeper into your faith. Every day during Advent I commit to taking one thing off my to-do list so that I can spend extra time in prayer and meditation. This keeps the season from being overcrowded and helps me focus on the task of examining my life in the light of His Word.

This Advent, as we remember Christ's coming to earth, we will take a deeper look at Who He is. We'll meditate on the names by which He has been identified to us in His Word and how each of those names gives us a glimpse of His nature, of His glory, and a glimpse of who we are meant to be in light of Who He is.

That the sovereign God of the universe has revealed Himself to us and wants us to know Him is a message of great hope, peace, joy, and love. During this time of year that can be so filled with busyness and activity, taking a few moments to speak His name will bring rest to our souls.

Truly, there's just something about that name—the name of Jesus.

Joseph was told by the angel who visited him, "you shall call His name Jesus, for He will save His people from their sins."

His name is the only name that brings redemption—the name that the Apostle Peter preached about when he said, "there is no other name under heaven by which men can be saved," and the name the Apostle Paul was talking about when he said, "whoever calls on the name of the Lord will be saved."

His name is the name that brings us comfort when we feel alone in our suffering and struggles as we call out to Him, our Emmanuel, the one Who is always with us.

It is the name that the world profanes, belittles, and blasphemes. For some, it is seen as a type of incantation—a magic word that brings about victory and prosperity. But it's the name that one day will send every knee to the ground as every tongue confesses that He is Lord to the glory of God.

For the next few weeks as we journey through this season of Advent together, we'll explore what this name means to those of us who love the Lord. We'll find great joy and peace in understanding what His name means to us in the context of our lives. We'll learn why His name should be treasured and honored, and, indeed, glorified, in our hearts and our lives.

This year, the proceeds from the Advent book project are being donated to a mission organization that does a great work in the United States and around the globe—GRASP International. The mission was originally started to reach people in Southern Peru with the Gospel of Jesus Christ. Over many years of hard work, the organization has expended to the entire country of Peru, Kenya, and Tanzania. Missionaries with GRASP are involved in church planting, seminary training, and building hospitals, Christian schools, and water filter factories. GRASP operates out of Arabi, Georgia, the location of Stillwater Pastor Retreat where pastors and their families can rekindle the fires of their passion for God and ministry as well as their love for each other. I'm grateful to be able to partner again this year with this mission organization as they labor to build the kingdom of God for the glory of His name.

December 1

THE KEY OF DAVID

O come, O Key of David, come
And open wide our heavenly home
Make safe for us the heavenward road
And bar the way to death's abode.
Rejoice, rejoice—Immanuel
Shall come to you, O Israel.

It is thought that the oldest Christmas carol we sing is "O Come, O Come, Immanuel." It was translated from Latin by John Mason Neal, who believed it was written in the 12th century. The song originated in what are known as the "seven O's," which are the great Advent prayers. Each of the seven prayers begins by addressing Christ by one of the names He is given in the Bible.

Jesus as known as the Holder of the Key of David, or simply, the Key of David, though this isn't one of His more commonly known names. But it's a beautiful name and crucial title, and one that He holds by virtue of His sovereignty and His power.

Revelation 3:7 tells us Christ is,

> *He who is holy, who is true, who has the key of David, who opens and no one will shut, and who shuts and no one opens...*

God is sovereign over absolutely everything. No matter what chaos, wickedness, or turmoil comes, He is ultimately in control. No matter how out of control this world is or becomes, we have great hope that our God, our Savior, is sovereign. Preacher A.B. Simpson said that Jesus is "King over nature, providence, the church, and the millennial world. " There is not a door He has ordained for you to enter that He cannot open.

Because He holds the key of David, Christ alone will decide who will enter the Kingdom of Heaven. And one day He will shut the gates of Hell for all eternity. But the precious promise behind this name is that those of us who belong to Him are drawn in close to Him and shut in. Just like Noah was shut into the ark, we are shut in, sealed, and safe with Him in His inner chambers where He gives us unspeakable joy and blessings.

This security means that we have nothing to fear because we know He's holding us close and hiding us away. It means we have no reason to be bound by worry or impatience. Imagine a child resting peacefully in his mother's arms, not struggling or fighting against her—that peace is what we have as we rest in our Father's arms, trusting He has a plan, trusting He is working out that plan no matter what our circumstances may look like.

I wonder, what would your life look like today if you were to place your complete faith in the Holder of the Key of David? Would the worry that creases your brow disappear? Would that fear for the future melt away? Would the frustration and impatience over the cares of the world be transformed into gratitude and peace for that hidden away place you can share with your Sovereign God?

Today, glorify His name, *the Holder of the Key of David.* Thank Him for His sovereignty. Thank Him for the hope that His sovereignty brings to your heart, and the security that comes from knowing that He is ultimately in control.

December 2

HALLOWED

Matthew 6:9-13; Luke 11:1-4

It was Vacation Bible School week and I was a young college student with a babysitting job during the summer. Every morning that week I would load my neighbors' two kids in my car and take them to the church, then bring them home and babysit them until their mom got home from work. Right after we arrived home from the church, we'd have lunch and then the kids, still pretty young, would retreat to their bedrooms for some time to play or read quietly.

It was the 80's and Nintendo's Mario Brothers video game had just been invented. Matthew, about 5 or 6 at the time, had a game console in his bedroom and opted to use his quiet time to advance in the game.

As I was reading in the living room I could hear his voice, somewhat muffled from his bedroom down the hall.

"Jesus! (mumble, mumble, mumble)."

"Jesus! (mumble, mumble, mumble)."

It was clear from his tone that he wasn't having a time of prayer. I quickly walked down the hall to his room. There he stood on top of his bed, game controller in his hand, repeating the mantra that was still a little garbled.

"Matthew," I exclaimed, "you shouldn't be saying Jesus' name like that!"

"The preacher says it," Matthew said, still intent on his game and paying me little attention.

"Which preacher?"

"The one at Bible School. He told us that when we ask God for help, we should always say this at the end…." And at this point in his explanation, and in the game, he said the words again:

"In Jesus' name, I play!" And, after a very intense moment of button mashing on his game controller, he explained, "I'm trying to get past this level, so I figured I'd ask God for help. In Jesus' name, I play!"

At first, I thought the lesson the pastor was trying to teach the VBS kids that summer was somehow lost on Matthew. But in reality, Matthew, with the innocence of a child, understood better than I did, that, because God is our Father, we can—and should—bring everything we do before Him in humble supplication for His help and blessing.

The passage of Scripture we know as the Lord's Prayer was taught on two occasions by Jesus. Once during the Sermon on the Mount, and once in response to His disciples' request that He teach them to pray. Both prayers are fairly similar, and both begin with addressing God as Father and giving honor to His name—"Hallowed be thy name.*" This term means to be set apart as worthy of honor and reverence. The Jewish people would have understood this, as some believed that God's name was too holy to be uttered, however, to pair the term "hallowed" with addressing God as "Father" had to seem somewhat challenging for them.

In our modern church culture, we can sometimes become so enamored with the thought of God as our Father that we forget He is a God who is to be honored, sanctified, and treated with reverence and honor like no other. In his article "Recovering Reverence," Dayo Adewoye writes,

> *In our fascination with God's love and mercy, we have lost sight of his majesty. In our excitement at God's*

approachability, we fail to sense his glorious power. Yes, we come to a loving God, but we forget he is a king. We have lost reverence for God.

Jesus taught us that God is approachable. We can address Him as our Father because Christ Himself came to secure that relationship on our behalf. But Jesus Himself honored His Father, and we are to do likewise. Addressing God as our Father should never diminish His glory, His hallowedness. Instead, it should draw us deeper into His holiness in a real and personal relationship that results in our being distinct reflections of His glory.

"Hallowed" is not a name by which we address God, it is a mindset. The Greek term used in Jesus' model prayer is a verb, and one of the meanings is "to separate from profane things, to consecrate, and to purify internally by renewing the soul." In other words, no matter by which name we approach our God, we are to do so with a recognition of the holiness, the sovereignty, and the power of the One we address. We are to approach Him with a willingness to honor Him, to glorify Him. We come into His presence not intending to have Him do our will but to have Him bend our wills to His.

Like my little friend Matthew, some use the name of Jesus as a magic word. We think, since we've prayed in His name surely He will give us what we want. We speak His name against temptation, against sickness, against financial difficulties, and we wonder why our circumstances don't improve. We've failed to grasp that approaching God in prayer is more about knowing Him and His will, and having Him change us, change our minds and our desires. It's about learning to stop offering Him suggestions about how to fix things, and instead just sit at His feet in humble quietness and worship, basking in Who He is.

Isaiah began his prophetic ministry with a vision of God. He describes the loftiness of the Lord, and the angelic creatures, the seraphim, that attended Him. Each seraph used two wings to cover his eyes because they would not dare to look directly at God's glory. Two wings covered their feet, signifying their lowliness, and with two wings they flew, always in movement to serve the Lord on His throne. All the while, the angels called out,

> *Holy, holy, holy, is the Lord of hosts. The whole earth is full of His glory.* (Isaiah 6)

John MacArthur says that, in this repetition of the word "holy" (a literary term known as "trihagion", or "thrice holy"), the angels affirm the character of God. He is never said to be love, love, love; goodness, goodness, goodness; mercy, mercy, mercy; or grace, grace, grace. He is always said to be holy, holy, holy.

Today, we are dwelling in a world that has turned the name of God, the name of Jesus, into profanity. We are guilty of using His name flippantly, and we have forgotten how to hallow His name. In a culture that wants to see God as only love, as only good, as only grace, etc., we must learn to first recognize Him as holy. I believe when God reveals Himself to us at His return, it will be His holiness that will bring all of mankind to our knees.

In coming to earth in the form of a man, I believe He wanted us to be confronted first with His holiness, and to see how His holy nature impacts every other characteristic that defines Him—and how His holiness also impacts us. Because of His holiness, there is great hope for our lives—hope for salvation, hope for sustaining grace during this life, and hope for spending all of eternity in His presence.

As we embark on this Advent journey to glorify His name, I hope we will be truly changed by remembering all that He is to us. I hope each of the names we read about will help us to understand Him better, to know Him more, and will transform us in eternal ways.

Today, as you consider how you can hallow His name, ask Him to give you a glimpse of His holiness, and a glimpse of His glory. Ask Him to give you a heart that truly knows how to approach each of His names with a purity of soul. Give Him glory today as you hallow His name.

December 3

ALPHA AND OMEGA

Revelation 21:5-6

Memories of Christmas always lead me back to my grandmother's house in South Mississippi. If you've read my book, Not Fit to Eat, you have already been introduced to Mama Dodds.

She was probably one of the most resourceful and creative women I've known. She was a master seamstress, at least in my opinion, and seemingly learned about feeding a crowd from Jesus' feeding the multitudes with five loaves and three fish.

One of the things Mama Dodds was known for was her work with a can of spray paint. Her philosophy was that a can of paint could make anything look brand new. We have a painted wooden rocking chair that came from her house. One summer after she passed away I decided to freshen the paint on it. I began painstakingly scraping the paint. I scraped the green and revealed red, I scraped the red and revealed a light blue, I scraped the light blue and revealed a brown. It was evident that she painted that chair a new color every year. Eventually, I gave up, gave the layer of paint I landed on a good sanding, and painted it white.

I suppose throughout the ages people have been doing the same thing. Currently, there is a trend among modern homemakers to buy thrifted or cast-off items and re-purpose them. A local thrift store I visit frequently, Re-new, is based on this very premise. Some things I've found there are perfect for my use as-is, while others need a little updating—like maybe a little spray paint. Re-new is operated by an organization called Women Reaching Our Community (WROC). Donations and sales at Re-New support the organization's mission of helping people in the community, many of whom are without a home. When I find a new treasure to "customize" for my home, I feel close to Mama Dodds, knowing that just maybe she passed on to me her passion for making old things new again.

In Revelation 1:8, Jesus calls Himself the Alpha and Omega. The Greek-speaking believers of the book of Revelation understood the reference to the first and last letters of the Greek alphabet. All their known language was found in that alphabet, just as our language is created from the letters of the English alphabet. By calling Himself Alpha and Omega, Christ was declaring that everything in the universe finds its fulfillment in Him. He is the first. He is the last, but He is also everything in between.

In Isaiah 43, God reminds us that there was no God before Him and there will be no God after Him. He is infinite and His existence defies the limits of time. But for us, His existence also defines the limits of our lives.

You see, He is Alpha and Omega of all things, but He is also Alpha and Omega of your life.

Psalm 139 is a beautiful portrait of how that works—how He has knit you together in your mother's womb, how He knows your every thought, how He is there with you no matter where you are, how He has ordained all of your days.

This name of God indicates to us that He has absolute control and creatorship over everything in existence—including you and me. Understanding this about God means that we also understand that, though He is unchanging, He is always about the business of transformation in our lives.

Isaiah records this message from the Lord,

Do not call to mind the former things, or ponder things of the past. Behold, I will do something new, now it will spring forth; Will you not be aware of it? I will even make a roadway in the wilderness, rivers in the desert... I have given waters in the wilderness and rivers in the desert, To give drink to My chosen people. The people whom I formed for Myself will declare My praise. (Isaiah 43:18-21)

This transformation begins with a change in us. No one understood this in the New Testament more clearly than the Apostle Paul. The transformation in His life is a powerful testimony to what God can do in each one of us. Paul went from being Saul the Pharisee intent on persecuting Christians to the point of death, to being Apostle Paul the missionary for Christ with one radically new goal.

Because Paul had personally experienced this radical change, he could encourage us with the truth that we don't have to remain the same. Though today's culture wants us to believe that we are "enough" and that the best thing we can do is accept ourselves the way we are, that type of teaching is not in line with Scripture. God wants to take the old self away from us and give us His new life. He wants to remove the burden we carry of having to be and feel "enough."

In Isaiah, He pictures the blessings He gives as streams of water in the desert. See, living on your own terms, your life is a spiritual desert— barren, dry. Materially you may have a nice home, expensive clothes, and enough money to buy what you want, but spiritually there is emptiness and in your quiet moments you sense it. No matter how much you have, no matter how many coats of paint you put on the outside, it's never enough—you feel that urge to have something more, something different.

The image of those streams of water comes back to us in Revelation 21,

Behold, I am making all things new.... It is done. I am the Alpha and Omega, the beginning and the end. I will give to

the one who thirsts from the spring of the water of life without cost.... (Revelation 21:5-6)

There is an unspoken contrast here between the "water of life" and the water the world offers. Matthew Henry describes worldly water this way: Sinful pleasures are muddy and poisoned waters, and the best comforts the world offers are like the dregs at the bottom of a cistern—the bring only frustration. But the joys that Christ gives are like waters springing from a fountain, pure, refreshing, abundant, and eternal. Jesus told the woman at the well in John 4 that all we need to do to have this water is to ask Him. The water He gives us "will become a well of water springing up to eternal life." It's water that will quench our thirst for all eternity. (John 4:7-14)

In the Bible, the wilderness is a picture of the place where God does this transforming work. According to author Andy Cook, there is a rabbinical saying in Israel that God has reserved the wilderness for Himself. When He wants to transform a person, He will often bring them into the wilderness. It was during the wilderness wanderings of the Israelites after He rescued them from Egypt that He taught His people how to be His people. Paul spent three years in the wilderness after His experience on the road to Damascus. And even Jesus sought the solitude of the wilderness before beginning His earthly ministry. It is in the wilderness that God teaches us how to love Him and trust Him, with all our hearts, soul, mind, and strength—because in the wilderness, He is all we have. It is in the wilderness that we learn to praise Him for Who He is and for what He is doing. When everything we have is stripped away, we can truly see His goodness and His glory.

The process may be difficult at times to understand, and God may not make our circumstances any better. But Scripture promises that not only has He begun a good work in us, but He will be faithful to complete it (Philippians 1:6).

God wants us to understand that, as our Alpha and Omega, He is with us when we enter the wilderness, and He is with us when we leave there—and He is there with us throughout that experience—transforming us. Through the hardest days, I encourage you to remember that He is doing an important work—renewing you to "the image of the One who created" you. (Colossians 3:10). It is this process of renewal that brings Him glory and honor.

He is with us because He loves us. He loved us from the first moment He conceived the thought of us and His love for us will never cease. Every moment of our existence, we are covered by His love, His grace, and His goodness—from the beginning to the end, and everything in between.

Take time to thank Him today that, no matter what you may be going through, you can trust that He is renewing you. Despite the circumstances you may be in today, He is making all things new. Though He may not change your circumstances, you can trust He is changing you to glorify Him through those circumstances. Thank Him that one day, upon His Second Advent, He will transform us in the twinkling of an eye, making us fit in an instance for eternity in Heaven with Him.

December 4

IMMANUEL

Isaiah 7:12-14

To many of us, there is not a more precious name for Jesus than the name Immanuel. It is this name that distinguishes Him as God with Us. This name brings comfort to us in times of loss, loneliness, and hardship. In fearful times—God is with us. In uncertain times-God is with us. In times of sickness and injury-God is with us.

The name of Immanuel was revealed to Isaiah by God in the context of His eventual destruction of the Assyrians and any other foreign powers who threatened the safety of His people. It was a fearful time in Judah, but God made a promise that their enemies wouldn't prevail. He commanded King Ahaz to ask Him for a sign that God was fighting with them. Ahaz refused, so God chose a sign for him.

Isaiah told Ahaz,

> Listen now, O house of David! Is it too slight a thing for you
> to try the patience of men, that you will try the patience of my
> God as well? Therefore, the Lord Himself will give you a
> sign; Behold, a virgin will be with child and bear a son, and
> she will call His name Immanuel. (Isaiah 7:12-14)

Matthew tells us that the name Immanuel means *God with us*. The name is a compound word that literally means "with us is God." And here's where the vocabulary-geek gets the better of me. The portion of the name that means God is *el*. This may be familiar to you. But the particular word used there is a form of the word "ayil," which can be translated as "ram. "

In the Old Testament, while a ram can be a form of sacrifice, as in the case of Abraham and Isaac, when God provided a ram, it could also be a sign of strength and victory. Jesus came as both. He willingly became the perfect sacrifice for the sake of fighting, and being victorious over, mankind's greatest enemy of all.

Over and over in Scripture, we see that the virgin birth isn't just a miraculous sign, though that does certainly qualify as a miracle. The miraculous nature is emphasized by the fact that, whenever God is seen triumphing on behalf of His people, it's in a way that no mortal man could possibly do.

Tony Evans has written that the name:

> *Immanuel originated within a context of pain, despair, loss, doubt, fear, and chaos. Immanuel came to a world in crisis. It is not merely a name to remember during Christmas while we sing carols and drink hot chocolate. No, Immanuel is a name of comfort when times are at their worst.*

Few of us can remember a worse time in modern US history than September 11, 2001. Stan Praimnath was there. He was standing at his desk on the 81st floor of the South Tower at 9:03 AM, talking to a friend from Chicago who had called to check on him. As he looked out his window toward the Statue of Liberty, he saw the Boeing 767 coming right toward him. He heard the screeching sound as the plane, flying 590 miles per hour, got closer. Stan recalls that,

> *With the jet just a few hundred yards from the South Tower, he dropped the phone and shouted, "LordIcantdothis. Youtakeover!"*

Eight words burst through his mouth like one word. He dove under his metal desk just as the plane hit the building.

Everything between floors 77 and 85 was destroyed, and 600 people were either killed or trapped. When Stan stood up, he saw his Bible was on his desk, undisturbed. Everything else was complete destruction.

Immediately Stan began to pray again, calling out for God to send someone to help him. He crawled through the rubble unable to find anyone—they had all been killed. Finally, he saw the light from a flashlight held by a man who was from the 84th floor and they were able to make their way out of the building.

As remarkable as Stan's account is, imagine the thousands of others that day who were also calling out to God—the ones who perished either in New York, Washington D.C., or a field in Pennsylvania. Imagine the millions of soldiers, victims of crime, victims of tragedies, throughout time who trusted God, cried to God, and still perished. Was Immanuel with them?

Perhaps one of the most comforting passages of Scriptures we have in our Bible is John 14. Its comfort lies in the fact that these are the words Jesus Himself spoke to His disciples before He left them for the cross of Calvary. These same words are for us. They speak of the depth of the loving and intimate relationship Jesus has with His disciples, of the mystery of how He can be physically absent from us but still very real, alive, and present. It's a passage of love, commitment, promise, and joyful fellowship. And amid all those promises, it's the promise of peace.

Jesus told them, and us,

> *Peace I leave with you; My peace I give to you; not as the world gives do I give to you. Do not let your heart be troubled, nor let it be fearful.* (John 14:27)

Believers are not immune to the trouble and tragedy in this world. We are, however, confident that God is with us always, because His Word promises it is so. We are confident that His very Spirit lives within us. We know this is true because He is the seal God has placed over our hearts. But there are times when our circumstances cause our flesh to be weak. Perhaps there are times when God allows us to experience the wilderness of hardship so that He can draw us closer to Himself.

Sometimes battles have to be fought for a long time before victory will come. But the name Immanuel promises victory to God's people. During those times we can remember that He is always with us, and He is always enough. We can rest in the promise of Immanuel—that miraculous sign that resonates through history—God is With Us.

Is there a battle or a burden you are facing today? Remember the many times throughout Scripture and your life when He has proven Himself to be Immanuel. In 2 Chronicles, God's people faced an insurmountable enemy with praise, and as they sang God's praises, He fought a victorious battle on their behalf. Maybe today is a good time for you to spend some time in praise for the victory God will one day win on your behalf. Glorify His name, Immanuel, today.

December 5

WONDERFUL

Psalm 106:7-8; Isaiah 9:6

Earlier this year I became concerned with how little recall I had of basic information. Like, how many times per second does a hummingbird flap its wings (50-80 by the way), or how much vinegar to use when you realize you only have regular milk and you need buttermilk (1 tablespoon per cup). When I was growing up, when questions like these arose in my little head, I would be told, "Look it up." And away I would go.

Of course, this was way before computers existed in homes, but there were always books in my house, and I would scour them trying to find the information I needed. First, I'd have to figure out which book to search. Then I'd have to figure out how to execute that search in whichever books I felt would have the answer. If the books in my house didn't include the information I needed, the second route I would take would be the phone-a-friend route. I learned as a child, and still hold to this crucial life-rule: Always have friends who are smarter than you are.

If no friend could give me the answer I needed, that meant a trip to the library. I'd start at the school library the next day, and if that turned up no leads, that would mean a trip to the library downtown. There, I would take my short pencil and scratch paper from the box on top of the card catalog, thumb through hundreds of cards, make a list of possibilities, and then use my scratch paper like a treasure map to navigate the shelves of the library.

Back then we needn't be in a hurry to find our answers. In the meantime, as we waited, there was something that happened in our little heads. We learned to think. We learned to ponder. We learned to imagine. We learned to wonder. Our minds entertained the unknown and as we did, we developed an appreciation for the process of thinking, pondering, imagining, and wondering. No, we didn't realize that's what we were doing, but this love for the process shaped us into people who can reason logically, who can appreciate the days of not knowing the answer, and how to patiently wait for the knowable to become known.

Now, there is Google. Or YouTube. Or TikTok. Google gave me 283,000 answers to my hummingbird question in .38 seconds. It took me longer to type the question than it did for the answers to populate. No time to ponder. Or think. Or imagine. Or wonder. Not only could I read about them, I could even see photos or videos about hummingbirds, and buy t-shirts, aprons, and wall-paper adorned with them.

The learning process, which led to enduring satisfaction and deeper engagement with information about the world, has been replaced with instant gratification. The brick library building with its shelves of thousands of books in all shapes, colors, and sizes, where I could interact with other seekers of information, has for many people been replaced with a tiny screen. The world, while literally at my fingertips, has lost its wonder.

It's at this time that Jesus, called Wonderful, has come. He is the only one Who can restore that sense of wonder to our lives. Old Testament words for wonder carry a variety of meanings—marvelous, extraordinary, miraculous, and separate. One author has said that one of the greatest benefits of wonder is that it allows us to sense in ourselves the greatness of God and the littleness of man. It's wonder that gives us a sense of depth and fulfillment, of joy and satisfaction with life.

Wiersbe wrote,

Whatever Jesus touched, He blessed and beautified, and made wonderful. He longed for people to open their eyes to see the world around them: the splendor of the lilies, the freedom of the sparrows, the miracle of the children, the message of the wind. He took everyday bread and wine and gave these necessities a depth of meaning that transformed them into luxuries of God's grace.

Job described the greatness of God to his friends by using examples of things that can be seen in the sky and on the earth—the weather, the sea, and the animals. He summed it all up with this,

Behold, these are the fringes of His ways; and how faint a word we hear of Him!

Though we can see His great power and understand in a limited way how His Creation works, He is too wonderful for us to completely understand.

Sometimes I think we are much like the Israelites who witnessed amazing wonders God performed on their behalf, but then just a few miles into the wilderness, they forgot. The Psalmist wrote,

Our fathers in Egypt did not understand your wonders...nevertheless, He saved them for the sake of His name that He might make His power known.

And also he reminds us to,

Give thanks to the Lord for His lovingkindness, and for His wonders to the sons of men! For He has satisfied the thirsty soul, and the hungry soul He has filled with what is good.

What does it take for you and me to see and enjoy Jesus as our Wonderful Savior? Especially at this time of the year, we must make time to spend with Him, and to see the world and this Advent season through His eyes. We must set aside time to think about God, to talk with Him, and to listen for His voice—and not as a mere curiosity that can be settled with a click of a button. Because He can't be. We can never understand all there is to know about Him, but the more we ponder Him, the more we will love Him, and the more we will want to continue to know Him and seek Him.

Do you know Him today as Wonderful? Can you glorify Him today in your life as your Wonderful Savior? Are you looking forward to that moment when you will see Him in all His glory and wonder, and stand in awe of Him as you finally see Him face to face?

December 6

COUNSELOR

Psalm 73:21-26; Isaiah 9:6

This morning I am wearing a particular brand and shade of nail polish I was inspired to purchase by Jennifer L. Scott, the Daily Connoisseur. I'm also very impressed with her approach to building her wardrobe based on only ten items per season. Including sleepwear. I just click the links in the information section of her YouTube channel, and I can go right to her Amazon store to find all the products she uses. Linda Davis, of New England Fine Living, has inspired me to reintroduce potpourri into my home and offers a variety of teas and pretty China cups for me to purchase in her store. She has also provided very convenient links for me to use that take me to her online store. Watching Midlife Stockman makes me want to go out and buy a particular brand of yard tools so I can tackle heavy yard chores really, really fast.

These are just three examples of the many social media influencers that tens of millions of us look to for lifestyle advice, political guidance, gaming, entertainment, and even spiritual counsel. They post their content as solutions to problems or answers to questions and then proceed to chat about their personal lives, sometimes narrating their daily activities, while highlighting products they use. It's a brilliant, though not original, marketing scheme, and those who do it well study the psychology of the consumer. They know their audience, they brand themselves well, and most of their viewers don't realize the money that changes hands. In 2024, the average social media influencer can make around $58,000 per year, while some of the more famous internet celebrities earn millions of dollars per post.

Followers of these influencers often feel a personal connection to them. As content revolves around common problems like fighting aging, decluttering a home, or weight loss, influencers exhibit their own struggles with vulnerability and emotion and then walk their viewers through how their problems are solved with a particular product.

God created us for relationships. Because of this, we all have an innate desire to be intimately known and understood. Even those people who always seem independent and confident and comfortable and strong have this need for relationships. We want people to understand and relate to the issues and problems we face and who can help us work out the answers to the deepest questions we encounter as we live our lives. And we can encounter some questions, can't we? We humans are messy beings and we often find ourselves in an almost urgent need for someone to intervene, to come alongside and help us.

So God sent Jesus whose name is Counselor.

One of the dictionary definitions of the term counselor is "one who advises, who serves as a consultant to help and lead others." In Isaiah 9, when the Messiah was identified as a counselor, the context was that of leading the nation of Israel and included military leadership. I find it very fascinating that among the five names in this passage that God gave His people to identify the Messiah, Counselor was one of them. He knew His people would need guidance—their own human counselors and advisors had failed them. Even the teaching of the prophets had been known to be poorly followed and, most likely, poorly interpreted on a personal and national level.

The counsel that Jesus brings us, however, is different. It's authoritative because it originates from the source—the very heart and mind of God

Himself. John 6 gives us an account of Jesus teaching in the synagogue in Capernaum. The teaching He was presenting was difficult, and some of those who had begun following Him became offended and discouraged—they chose to turn back. Jesus turned to the twelve men He had chosen and asked,

> *What about you? Do you want to leave me?*

Simon Peter answered him,

> *Lord, to whom shall we go? You have the words of eternal life. We have come to believe and to know that you are the Holy One of God.*

Jesus' role as our Counselor is so important in our world today. There truly are so many voices all around us, and each one has to be carefully weighed against His Word. These voices are often quick to distract us from the ultimate purpose the Lord has for us. They are quick to excuse our sins as "mistakes" or poor behavior. They can smoothly water down the decrees of God into mere suggestions. If we are not careful with the counselors we choose to listen to, we will soon fall into the trap of idolatry and even self-worship.

I love what one writer has said about Jesus as our Counselor,

> *Your counselor knows the decisions you must make and how important those decisions are to you and to Him. God is lovingly wrapped up in your life. He has a tremendous investment in your future.*

He goes on to say that even in the mundane things of life we should seek His counsel. And as we do so, we get to know Him better, and can better understand His will.

But what if you've gotten off track? Perhaps you have gotten mired down by worldly counselors who have led you down a path away from God's

Word. Perhaps the world's voices have lured you away from the counsel found in the Word and you feel drawn ever farther outside of God's will for you today.

May I gently suggest that you turn those voices off? If you have replaced turning the pages of your Bible with scrolling your social media screens, turn off those screens. And my friends, if you have joined the ranks of the modern Bible readers who use a Bible app on your tablet or phone, please get a real Bible. It's so simple, with the tap of a finger, to toggle the Bible app with TikTok. Or when we get to a verse we don't understand, we can ask ourselves what our favorite spiritual influencer says about that passage—and instead of getting lost in the pages of the Word of God, we find ourselves getting lost in the pages of the Internet. Maybe your influence is the twenty-four-hour news media, which gives us an hour of news and spends twenty-three hours in excruciatingly detailed opinions about the news. Just turn it off.

What's the danger of it, you ask? It's entertainment, you declare. The danger comes when we expose our hearts and our minds to the thoughts and opinions of others who can very well draw us away—they are men and women who want to fill the role of a counselor in our lives, not for our benefit, but for their own financial gain.

In Psalm 73, the songwriter shares how he had almost lost his footing— he watched how the wicked and arrogant, those "influencers" of his day who didn't follow God, were prospering and he thought he would follow their ways. He says of these people,

> *Their mouths lay claim to heaven, and their tongues take possession of the earth. Therefore their people turn to them and drink up waters in abundance....*

He came to believe,

Surely in vain I have kept my heart pure and have washed my hands in innocence. All day long I have been afflicted, and every morning brings new punishments.

But soon God reminded him,

Yet I am always with you; you hold me by my right hand. You guide me with your counsel, and afterward, you will take me into glory. Whom have I in heaven but you? And earth has nothing I desire besides you. My flesh and my heart may fail, but God is the strength of my heart and my portion forever.

During this Advent season, reconnect with Jesus as your Counselor. Turn off the voices that would lead you away from Him. Let Him guide you and advise you, no matter what the world throws at you. Yes, sometimes we find His words can be difficult. But He stands ready to lead us. He will give you the ability to trust Him and to obey His Word even when life is hard. Glorify His name, Counselor, today.

December 7

PRINCE OF PEACE

John 14:27

Today you are reading about Jesus as our Prince of Peace. Before we get into this topic, let me share with you how it's going with me.

My life has been short on peace lately. So, as soon as I got a break, my husband and I traveled to Darien, Georgia, which is where I take my annual writing retreat. I've written before about JoAnn and David—the hosts of the bed and breakfast where I've been staying for a few years, and now where my husband is joining me. We truly love being here, and if there is anywhere I can find peace, it's here on the porch outside my room, watching the sun stroll across the marsh and listening to the birds.

When I got up this morning, Dave and JoAnn were watching the financial news as stocks all over the world seem to be crashing—the media is calling it Bloody Monday. I quickly retreated to our room, put some Christmas worship into my noise-canceling headphones, and wrote a few more pages before breakfast. Later, it was time for another break. I ventured out into the living room where Mike was working on a jigsaw puzzle. The news was on in the background with all sorts of warnings about an imminent attack on Israel by Iran. Again, I retreated into our room, but by this time, my spirit was too grieved to write.

I went back to the living room and told Mike it was time for me to get a change of scenery. This is not an unusual part of my writing retreat, and

Darien has such beautiful views of the marsh and the river, so taking a drive to soak in the coastal ambiance is always a good way to clear my mind when I get a little stuck.

Off we go on a little drive. Perhaps I should mention we are sitting in the middle of Tropical Storm Debby which has been pouring rain on us most of the day and tossing our vehicle around on the roads. Right—on a day when I need the coastal equivalent of a quaint Christmas village where we can get snowed in by a blizzard and sip cocoa by a roaring fire like in those Hallmark Christmas movies, we are watching for flooded roadways and downed power lines.

After our abbreviated sight-seeing venture, we pulled back into the driveway of the bed and breakfast. I couldn't help but chuckle. Here I am, trying to find a way to soothe my spirit and calm my thoughts that have been stirred up by the fearful circumstances in our world so that I can dig into the Scriptures and write about the glory of the name of our Prince of Peace. Isn't it just like the Lord to send me running right to Him? Only He can truly minister that peace to our hearts—He just had to give me a vivid reminder of that today.

I think we all have been encouraged by the truth that Jesus brings us peace, unlike any other peace the world offers. It's a peace that brings comfort, a sense that there is nothing or no one at odds with us. It is a peace that means we are made right with God, no longer His enemy.

But when we speak of this glorious name—the Prince of Peace—we are speaking of the role of Jesus as the promised ruler over His people who brings an end to the war and conflict that has always plagued them. War will end under this Ruler and the promise made to David in 2 Samuel 7 will be fulfilled. Read the words to this promise,

> *I will make you a great name, like the names of the great men who are on the earth. I will also appoint a place for My people Israel and will plant them, that they may live in their*

own place and not be disturbed again, nor will the wicked afflict them any more as formerly, even from the day that I commanded judges to be over My people Israel; and I will give you rest from all your enemies.

In a real sense, this promise won't be completely fulfilled for us until Jesus establishes His eternal Kingdom. But our Savior who will be Prince of Peace in eternity is still our Prince of Peace today. As you consider this promise, I wonder what enemy you are seeking rest from today. Ultimately, the enemy of our souls, Satan, who is the temporary ruler of this world, is at the heart of the conflict that creates fear and worry and every evil thing. He works hard to orchestrate the circumstances of world events, and life events, to distract us from the power and righteousness of Christ.

Later in Isaiah 26, we read,

The steadfast of mind You will keep in perfect peace because he trusts in You. Trust in the Lord forever, for in God the Lord, we have an everlasting Rock

So when we are experiencing days when our hearts are stirred up within us and we are fearful for what our future brings, we can retreat to that place of refuge where our Prince of Peace comforts us with the truth that one day He will put an end to all our conflict—he will establish a kingdom of peace for us.

In this world, we can never experience the fullness and completeness that God's peace will one day afford us. We can work at being people of peace while standing firm for righteousness. We can strengthen our spirits to weather life's storms with grace, dignity, and honor. And we can speak the peace of Christ into the hearts of the people we cross paths with. But in a very real sense, that peace is lacking something. Still, we have hope.

Henry Wadsworth Longfellow lost his beloved wife in 1861 when an accident with a candle caught her nightgown on fire. Two years later, his son was severely wounded in a Civil War battle. Longfellow poured out his heart into a poem, now set to music as a familiar Christmas carol that encourages us that, while we will experience tragedy upon tragedy and conflict upon conflict in this world, we have a future hope for the peace that the angels proclaimed the night Jesus was born,

> *And in despair, I bowed my head;*
> *"There is no peace on earth," I said;*
> *"For hate is strong,*
> *And mocks the song*
> *Of peace on earth, good-will to men!"*
>
> *Then pealed the bells more loud and deep:*
> *"God is not dead, nor doth He sleep;*
> *The Wrong shall fail,*
> *The Right prevail,*
> *With peace on earth, good-will to men."*

Today as you glorify the name of your Prince of Peace, give Him thanks for the hope you have for the day his Kingdom will be established. Thank Him for the grace, mercy, and comfort He gives you as you daily encounter a world that brings fear and turmoil. Because of the hope you have for His imminent second Advent, you can face the obstacles of life with peace, knowing He carries you on His very able shoulders.

December 8

LORD

Away in a manger, no crib for a bed
The little Lord Jesus laid down His sweet head
The stars in the sky looked down where He lay
The little Lord Jesus asleep in the hay.

This is probably one of the first Christmas carols Sunday School children learn to sing. It's a simple melody with simple words, and it has really cute motions for busy children to have something to do with their hands while singing in front of the congregation. In fact, the song first appeared in a children's Sunday School booklet published by the Lutheran church back in 1885, with no known source for the lyrics. That initial publication included only two stanzas, with two more added later.

The repetition of the phrase *Little Lord Jesus* is comforting to little hearts. To think this Jesus they are learning to love was once a baby, just like they were babies. To think of Him as a toddler, learning to brush His teeth and tie His sandals—just like them—makes Him somehow more real to them. It makes Him seem accessible to them. And maybe if we are all honest, it makes Him seem accessible to us grown-ups, too.

In coming to earth as a baby, He did become accessible to us. He did so in order to bring the glory of God down here among mankind. Even though He walked among men, not one bit of His glory was diminished. Not one bit of His Lordship.

If you are taking the time to read this devotional during this busy season of the year, my guess is that you don't need the Lordship of Jesus explained to you. You already understand that He is to be your Lord, your Master. You know that you are to follow Him in growing obedience and devotion.

What does His Lordship look like in your life today? Are you fully living as a yielded, surrendered, servant of the Most High God? Are you growing closer to Him day by day? Are you digging deep into His Word every day to know Him better so that you can hear His voice more clearly? Are there relationships or habits you've picked up along the way that would not be glorifying to your Lord?

Every day we live as followers of Jesus, we learn a little bit more about what it means to honor Him as our Lord. We learn that all our resources—money, vehicles, homes, jobs, relationships—are on loan to us. We learn that He has a specific purpose for these things, and for our time and talents while we are here on this earth—and that purpose is that we use them to glorify God.

Today as you glorify His name, Lord, ask Him to show you where your heart may not be fully surrendered to Him. Ask Him to give you wisdom, His wisdom, to know how to use all that He's given you for His honor and glory. Thank Him that He is your Lord.

December 9

BREAD OF LIFE

John 6:31-35

One of the things I love about the Christmas season is the opportunity it gives me to bake. I love getting in the kitchen and inhaling all the aromas of the holiday season—the cinnamon, nutmeg, ginger—all those warm spices that seem to make the house feel brighter and more welcoming. This year I have been baking a lot of our bread at home, so I'm eager to try some of the traditional Christmas breads from around the world. One of those is *stollen,* which is a traditional German bread enjoyed during Advent. Originally in the late 1300's, the bread was only made with flour, oats, and oil, because of the requirement for German Catholics to fast from animal-derived ingredients during Advent. But in the late 1400s, German bakers had a serious word with the pope, and he removed the ban.

Stollen today is a yeast bread with fruit, nuts, and marzipan. It's brushed with lots of sweet butter and rolled into a cylinder which is said to make the loaf resemble the Christ Child wrapped in swaddling cloths. Often you will see it referred to as Chrisstollen because of this shape. We shall see if I can pull this one off!

Jesus called Himself the Bread of Life, and this was significant for several reasons. Bread was a common theme in Scripture because it was the basic substance of the Israelites' daily meals. We are familiar with the manna that God sent to the Israelites on six days of the week as they wandered

49

in the wilderness. And in the familiar Lord's Prayer, we're taught to ask God to provide our daily bread. In the Temple, the bread of the Presence was kept on a special gold table. This bread signified God's continual communion with His people.

After Jesus fed the 5,000, many from that crowd followed Him. Jesus saw this as a teaching opportunity and pointed out to them that they were simply following Him because they had eaten the meal He had provided. They were satisfied with a full stomach but had missed the miraculous sign He had performed that showed He was the Messiah. This proved to be a hard truth for them to understand. The people wanted to know what they needed to do to work for the food that He offered. Jesus replied that He is the Bread of Life. Having faith and believing in Him as the Son of God would allow them to partake of this bread that would give them eternal life.

Still, the people couldn't see past their physical hunger to understand the eternal spiritual emptiness that Jesus was offering to fill, an emptiness that only Jesus could fill. They had seen Him divide five loaves of bread and two fish to feed 5,000 people. There could have been 5,000,000 people and still those few loaves and fish would have been enough. They didn't have to grow the grain, or bake the bread—they only had to partake. And Jesus wanted them to understand that He was enough—His sacrifice would be enough for all of mankind. He is the bread of life—the bread of eternal life.

I was reminded of those 5,000 today when I read a story about Mike Meaders. Mike runs a boiled peanut and produce stand in Cleveland, Georgia, in White County. He calls it the "kids thing" and he started in 2017, collecting donations from customers by asking them to throw their change into a container dedicated to paying off student lunch debt in White County. Over the past seven years, Mr. Meaders has donated about $16,000 to various elementary schools in White County. As the writers of the article point out, "A burden shared is a burden halved, by cracking open a peanut." Mr. Meaders says this about his "kid thing,"

It makes you feel good. I think it's God's work in a way. Well, I know it is."

There are a lot of hungry stomachs in our world, but more so than physical hunger, there is great spiritual hunger in our world. So many people strive to find something that will satisfy the hunger they have. The world offers us a lot of substitutes for that Bread of Life, things to fill that inner emptiness. People build mansions, thinking a nice home will satisfy them. Then they spend their time traveling all over the world, thinking experiences will satisfy them. Some people look for ways to serve their communities, thinking the good feeling that comes from helping will satisfy them. But the truth is, only Jesus, only the Bread of Life, will fulfill us, only He will satisfy us.

Today, glorify His name—the Bread of Life. Thank Him for the sacrifice of His body that has bought you eternal life. Thank Him for the bread of His presence, that He is always in communion with you. As Christmas approaches, and you meditate about His birth in Bethlehem, the House of Bread, think of ways you can share this Bread of Life with others who need to know the satisfaction that only He can give.

December 10

THE WORD

John 1:1-14

It was the stand-by classroom time-killer game for the day before Christmas break: How many words, using at least 4 letters, can you make with the letters of Merry Christmas? I don't remember the exact total, but I believe it's somewhere between 1,600 and 2,000. Middle school kids, the age I taught for many years, aren't real keen on word games, but when you make it a competition, you can kind of keep them engaged. One year, I had a particularly rowdy bunch, so I made it into a relay race where the 20 or so students in my class formed two teams. They lined up in their teams at the back of the classroom, then at my signal would run, one at a time, to the board, write a word, then run back and tag the next person. The catch was each team appointed a word monitor for the competing team. They would either give the words a thumbs up or a thumbs down based on whether an actual, "legal," word was used. That was always good for ending the first half of the school year, and sending the kids off on their Christmas holidays, with a good argument.

Words are important. Of course, they are how we communicate our thoughts, our questions, our ideas. The fact that we are created for the use of common language signifies that we are created for relationships, for it is with the use of words that relationships are formed and built.

God used His spoken word to bring everything into creation, and throughout Scripture, we see the importance of God using His words to communicate with His people. In John's Gospel, he identifies that Jesus was the embodiment of that Word of creation. He was there with God in the very beginning and was sent forth even then as the Word of God. This shows us that Jesus has always enjoyed intimate companionship with God the Father. Isaiah 55:11 tells us that every word that goes forth from Him will accomplish whatever He pleases, and won't return to Him void, but will prosper. When we think of the work that Christ did in accomplishing our redemption, we understand the dept of the truth of that verse.

In John 1:14 we read that the Word became flesh and dwelt among us. The word "dwelt" actually means he "tented, or tabernacled," and this was a reminder to God's people of the Tabernacle that symbolized God's presence with them in the wilderness. This time was different. God Himself, in the form of a man, dwelt with them. He walked with them and worked alongside them, taught them in the synagogue, and had conversations over meals with them. When the time came, He died a very public death that would not end in the grave, but with His resurrection. And as all of that played out, they saw the glory of God.

Now, for us, it is through the written Word of God that He reveals His truth to us. Reading and studying Scripture, while it seems a chore to some people, is a privilege. That Word holds comfort and joy, it reminds us of the path God has mapped out for us in being people who glorify Him. His Word teaches us to pray, to battle spiritual enemies, and to rest in His authority and power. His Word gives great encouragement as we are assured of His ultimate victory over all the evil and wickedness in this world, over the powers of hell and the devil who tries to destroy and devour us.

Advent reminds us that we are waiting to hear His voice. We are told that He will return with a shout. It will be a battle cry. Revelation describes to us that at the final battle, there will be a sword that comes forth from His mouth—so it could be that it is the sword of the Spirit, the Word of God, that, just as He spoke the world into being, He will speak and this sin-ravaged world will be destroyed, making way for the new Heaven and the new Earth.

Today, glorify the name of Jesus the Word. Let His word dwell richly in you so that you can know the depth and intimacy of companionship with Him. Ask God to reignite your heart for His Word, ask Him for a renewed mind to understand, a new hunger to open and explore, and a stronger curiosity about what His Word has to say to you. Glorify Him today as the Word of God.

December 11

THE VINE

John 15:1-11

Which is easier to do—pray for an hour, or use that same hour for scrolling social media? Is it easier to spend 30 minutes reading a passage of Scripture, or 30 minutes "researching" something trivial on your smart phone? Maybe that's an unfair question because we all know the spiritual disciplines of prayer, meditation, and Scripture reading are called "disciplines" for a reason. But what about a conversation with a friend? How many times have I witnessed friends or families or couples at restaurants, noses to screens, barely glancing at one another because whatever is happening on those tiny screens in their hands has their attention captivated?

One author has described these screen worlds that have us so firmly in their power as *disembodied, virtual worlds where users broadcast to a crowd* instead of developing one-on-one, face-to-face relationships. This lack of connection with one another has brought about a sense of loneliness, isolation, and even a sense of confusion and lostness when it comes to making important decisions in life.

It is into this world of artificial connections where the human soul finds no true satisfaction, that Jesus speaks His name, The Vine. It's a beautiful picture of what it means to be connected to Him, and through Him to God the Father. We are branches who are fed, nourished, and at times pruned so that we will naturally bear fruit that brings Him glory.

When I think about being so intimately connected to Jesus, the Vine, in comparison, any other connection I may have dims. Nothing else matters.

In this passage of John 15, Jesus takes the time to contrast fruitful branches against the unfruitful branches. The branches that bear fruit are those of us who are truly saved, whose lives are characterized by constant abiding in Him and with Him. We stay connected to Him, that is, we abide in Him in love, through His Word, through prayer, and by obedience. And the result, He tells us, is that His joy will dwell in us, making our own joy full.

Some branches don't bear fruit. These are people who may claim to be Christians, but who have never truly experienced salvation. They wither away and are burned up. Their fruitlessness is because they are not joined to the vine. Without that true connection, without salvation, they can't have the nourishment that comes to our lives through His.

It is quite interesting to note in this passage that bearing fruit is not what is commanded for believers. We are commanded to *abide*. It is understood that as we abide, our lives will naturally bear fruit. And when we are fruitful, God will be glorified.

Sometimes fruitful abiding can be difficult to do. It requires a commitment to spend time with the Lord, and to do that we have to change some habits that our flesh dearly loves. We put a lot of stock these days in our "down-time." We like to spend our weekends traveling even when it takes us out of church. We like to keep up with our favorite television series, even though it exposes us to darkness and godless ideas. We like to sleep a few extra minutes in the morning instead of getting up and sticking to our scheduled time with the Lord.

As branches connected to Jesus, the Vine, our habits must change if we are going to be fruitful. Yes, there is a discipline to learning to abide. That discipline requires us to quiet the desires of our flesh that pull us away from time with Him. Those things may give us temporary entertainment and temporary, earth-bound memories, but those are things that don't nourish our souls. Abiding in Him means that His life nourishes us. His words will become our words. His ideas will become our ideas. His love for others will become our love for others, and His joy will become our joy.

As we approach Christmas and the New Year, maybe it's a good time for you to consider how firmly connected you are to the Vine. Are you abiding in Him? Can you go a little deeper with Him in the coming year? Today as you glorify the name of The Vine, ask Him to give you a fresh sense of connection to Him. Ask Him to give you the grace to use the precious moments of your life to spend abiding in Him. Thank Him for allowing you to bear fruit for Him, and thank Him for the joy that He promises to give. May you experience that fullness of joy today.

December 12

THE GREAT PHYSICIAN

Mark 2:1-17

Since 1995 I have struggled with an autoimmune disease that causes a lot of random symptoms that seem to have no explanation. The symptoms are caused by elevated levels of certain antibodies that most doctors don't want to check for. One doctor told me there's nothing that can ever be done about it, so why waste the time tracking it? Needless to say, like everyone else, I've had to learn to be my own advocate when it comes to doctors. When I was in my 30's and 40's, I saw a doctor in town pretty regularly for wellness visits. We'd go through the usual stuff—labs, blood pressure, EKG, etc. Then he'd look in my throat, and with a very concerned expression he'd say, "We really need to talk about getting those tonsils out." To which I'd very graciously thank him for his concern and assure him that I would think about it. Of course, I plan on taking those tonsils with me when I leave this earth, but I never told him I had no intention of having them removed.

My annual wellness checks always fell around the late January-mid-February time frame. In February of 2017 I went through the normal exam, but this time it was different. Instead of looking into my throat with his usual concern, this time, he focused on another part of my anatomy. You see, in January of 2017, I turned 50. Tonsils were child's-play. Now, it was time for us to schedule my colonoscopy.

"But what about my tonsils," I asked innocently.

"Your tonsils are fine," he responded dismissively. I'm still not sure how one birthday can make my tonsils perfectly healthy, but I'm content to keep them.

Obviously, everyone wants a doctor who is competent in their profession. But there is a lot to be said for a doctor with the type of bedside manner who can keep you optimistic even in the face of bad, or even devastating news. We want doctors who listen and who make us feel known. We want doctors who treat us as real people. I suppose when it comes to the doctor I'm seeing now, the thing I like the most about her is that she doesn't just *treat* her patients. She *cares* for them.

Jesus is called the Great Physician because of His words in Mark 2. This chapter is familiar as it involves the story of a man who was paralyzed and then healed by Jesus when the man's four friends lowered him through a hole in the roof. First, Jesus tells the man his sins are forgiven. After a heated discussion with the religious leaders present, Jesus tells the man to get up, take his pallet, and go home. But this is not when Jesus refers to Himself as a physician.

Following the account of the paralytic is the story of when Jesus called Levi, or Matthew, to be His disciple. Levi was a dishonest tax collector, but when Jesus looked at him and said, "Follow Me," the Bible says that he got up. These were the same words used for the paralytic who was healed and "got up." Later, when the religious people were complaining about Jesus dining with Matthew, the tax collector, Jesus spoke these words,

> It is not those who are healthy who need a physician, but those who are sick; I did not come to call the righteous, but sinners.

When Matthew got up and followed Jesus, it was because he knew he needed the redemption Christ offered. When we consider the work of Advent, of preparing for the arrival of our Savior, a very important part of that is recognizing and repenting of any sin in your life, and any distance you may have put between yourself and your Savior.

We must remember the most deadly disease Jesus came to heal is the disease that leads to eternal death. He doesn't just heal us, though, He truly cares for us. He truly loves us and wants to draw every sinner to repentance and wholeness through Him. One author has written,

> *Spiritual blindness to our own condition must be overcome if we are to be saved from sin. As long as we do not believe we are sinners, we cannot receive the cure, for only those who know they need a cure will receive it. In order to move closer to God, we first have to confess how far away we are from Him.*

During the COVID pandemic, there was a marked increase in consumer spending on comfort items. As fear and uncertainty seemed to reign, people were drawn to comfort foods, soft and comfortable clothes, pajamas, and blankets. There was also a trend toward things like sewing, knitting, and gardening. Studies were conducted during this time to show how the brain was impacted by various ad strategies at the height of the pandemic, and it was shown that this was a matter of people looking for some sense of control during a time when the world seemed out of control.

We still see this trend today as industries respond to the rising stress and uncertainties that continue across our globe. At the same time as people continue their pursuit of comfort—investing time and money to find that security they are missing, we are also seeing a decline in church attendance and a loss of basic Biblical knowledge. We are seeing many who are walking away from their faith and a rapid increase of darkness in our world. There is a spiritual connection here that should not be missed. People are seeking comfort in things that can never bring comfort. They are seeking healing and goodness in disposable things. It seems the more we seek comfort and security in things that are passing away, the darker the world is becoming.

Gloomy outlook? Yes, unless we look up, into the eyes of the Great Physician. The One who tells us to get up and follow Him. To forsake this world and the things of it that can never heal, cure, comfort, or satisfy. To recognize the utter hopelessness that is offered by the things in this world, and to embrace the pure hope He offers. As author Jen Wilkin so aptly writes, we can't,

> *Create hope where there is hopelessness… but we can cry out to the God who can.*

She goes on to say,

> *Not everything will be made new in this lifetime, but His promise to grow in us the fruit of the Spirit means we can know abundant life whether circumstances heal or not.*

There is great hope for us during this season of Advent in knowing Jesus Christ as our Great Physician. If sin, uncertainty, or the cares of this world have taken hold of your hands, your feet, your thoughts, your emotions, or your mouth, leaving you spiritually paralyzed in some way, today is the day to confess, to get up, and move closer to Him. He so dearly wants to draw you close to Him. He truly cares for you like no other can.

Today as you glorify His name, The Great Physician, give Him praise for redeeming you and saving you. Give Him thanks for drawing you into a place of spiritual healing and wholeness, for giving you hope amid uncertainty and peace amid turmoil.

December 13

RABBI

Isaiah 30:18-21; Matthew 11:28-30

As Christmas rapidly approaches, you may often find me in the kitchen baking all sorts of cookies that will be packed into fun or pretty baskets with other fun delicacies. I really love to bake, but ironically, I'm not that crazy about eating all the sweet treats I make. Fortunately, I have friends who do like to eat them!

Over the years I've spent a lot of time in the kitchen. It was my grandmother, Mama Dodds, who taught me to cook and bake. I don't know if she passed on her love for cooking to me during those hot summers I spent in her tiny kitchen, or if I came equipped with that in my DNA, but she did teach me many skills and simple principles I still remember today. My book, *Not Fit to Eat* is a book of family recipes, and the memories that accompany them, that have been passed down from Mama Dodds, my mom, and my two aunts.

Michelle Gowan, a retired school teacher from Bonaire, Georgia, picked up on the legacy of teaching younger cooks the kitchen ropes and founded the Cookie School. She even developed her own signature baking extract—Cookie Nip. At her home kitchen-based cookie classes, students will mix, roll, bake, frost, and decorate their own cookies. They'll take home a pan, a "secret recipe" for cookies, and a bottle of Cookie Nip. Several of my friends have joined in the fun of this and learned to make amazing cookies. What better way to "make spirits bright" this Christmas than by baking up a pan of cookies for family and friends?!

I'm sure all of us have special people in our lives who were important to us because of what they taught us. As a child, I thought my teachers were the biggest celebrities in the world! I looked up to them, respected them, and wanted to be like them. If I needed help or assurance, I went to them. I wanted to make them proud of me—and honestly, I still do.

Because of the love I had for my teachers and how important they were, and still are, to me, I completely understand Mary Magdalene's one-word response when she met the risen Christ outside the empty tomb. Though she had been speaking to Him, she didn't recognize Him until He spoke her name. When He did, she turned and said to Him, "Rabboni," which is a word that means Teacher, or Master. The term Rabboni carries with it an emphasis that means *my great Master* or *my great Teacher.* I think in that moment this word was both a title and an endearment.

Why is it so important that we know Jesus as our *Rabbi*? For years, God's people had been unfaithful to Him, despite His goodness and faithfulness to them. In Isaiah 30:18, they were reminded that God longs to be faithful to them, and He *waits on high to have compassion* on them. As older generations died out and newer ones were born, God's people gradually forgot how to actually be His people. Even if they had a desire to be obedient, they needed someone to show them how.

This passage goes on to say,

> *Although the Lord has given you bread of privation and water of oppression, He, your Teacher, will no longer hide Himself, but your eyes will behold your Teacher. Your ears will hear a word behind you, 'This is the way, walk in it,' whenever you turn to the right or to the left.*

During Jesus' earthly ministry, He taught in synagogues, in fields, in boats, and on roads. He taught at dinner tables, in living rooms, and in the wilderness. He taught with conversation, with stories, with parables, with miracles, with how He lived, and with how He died. He was truly the great, master Teacher.

Just as any great teacher does, He taught what He knew, and knew what He taught. Jesus was fully God, so He was able to teach us about God. He was able to show us God. In John 14, Jesus told His disciples that because they had seen Him, they had seen the Father. But Jesus was also fully man, so He was able to teach us more about ourselves than any other teacher ever could. He taught us how to relate to God by turning away from sin and wickedness and living lives of devotion and reverence to God. He taught us how to seek God through prayer. And He taught us how to relate to one another, by putting others' needs above our own, by showing selfless love, by serving and washing feet.

He taught us, and He encouraged us, to be like Him,

> *Come to me, all who are weary and heavy-laden, and I will give you rest. Take My yoke upon you and learn from Me, for I am gentle and humble in heart, and you will find rest for your souls. For My yoke is easy and My burden is light.*
> Matthew 11:28

In this passage, Jesus is quoting Jeremiah 6, which is a picture of travelers who have allowed themselves to be led astray and are lost. They are stopping and seeking direction, trying to find the "ancient paths" that will lead them back in the right direction—back to God. So here in Matthew, Jesus is telling us that *He* is the one Who will teach us the right way. And He will not only show us the way, but if we make Him our Master Teacher, if we yoke ourselves to Him, He will lead us in gentleness and meekness.

Today as you glorify His name, Rabbi, thank Him for all the ways He gently leads you through this life. Perhaps you have wandered away from Him or been led astray. Today He is asking you to come to Him, to learn from Him. Ask Him for the faith you need to do that. Give Him praise today as your *Rabboni*, your great Master, and your Teacher.

December 14

I AM

John 8:54-58

I have to admit, no matter how old I am, I am always going to be a kid at Christmas time. I love decorating the house to the nines, putting up the tree and decking it all out, and keeping the house full of soft and festive music. Each year you can be sure, I'm going to wrap every package as fancy as I can, and I will make sure that Mike's stocking is overflowing. Though I'm writing these pages in the heat of summer, I've got a closet filled with gifts ready to be sorted and placed under the tree.

One of the things I love about observing the season of Advent is that it allows me to approach the season of Christmas with a sense of slowing down to gaze into the face of my Savior, instead of getting so wrapped up in the traditional Christmas celebrations and activities that I forget to think of Him.

In slow and prayerful gazing, my soul comes to realize that there is more to Him than I can ever understand. There is so much fullness to His being that I can never capture it all in a single glance. Every day, every moment, I find something new, and I understand more and more that He is everything I will ever need.

Today we consider the glory of the name I Am and I find myself almost at a loss for words. How do I take this name that encompasses everything

God is, everything that Jesus came to be, and boil it down into just a few words?

The word translated I Am is YHWH and it's referred to as the tetragrammaton—that's a long word that is defined as "The Four Letters." Translated into Hebrew, the name becomes Yahweh. Translated into English, it is Jehovah. This is the name that means the "covenant-keeping relational God."

From the instant He was conceived by the Holy Spirit in the womb of Mary His mother, Jesus carried around with Him the identity of I Am. This name, by which God identified Himself to Moses, encompasses every aspect of existence—what was, what is, what will come, and it was the name He used to explain who He is in relationship to man.

He was God who came down from Heaven to accomplish the work of the covenant of redemption. As a man, He was the human form of everything that God is, but He was accessible to man. Tony Evans writes,

> *Without Jesus, we cannot know God's heart, His person, or His character intimately because He is wholly other and sits outside our realm of understanding.*

As human beings bound by the physical world, we cannot see God. Because He wanted to be seen by us, He had to come to us in the form of a man. This is what we call the incarnation. And because of this, John wrote that mankind was finally able to see His glory,

> *glory as of the only begotten of the Father, full of grace and truth.*

I Am, therefore, is the name that brought God and man into a relationship with one another. There is glory in that name, there is authority and power in that name. There is provision for our every need in that name. There is redemption and an eternal, indestructible inheritance for His children in that name. There is assurance in the name I Am that every need you have is already met. He is, indeed, everything we could ever need, both for now and for all eternity.

As you glorify the name I Am today, there is so much to be thankful for. As your preparations in your home bring you closer to Christmas, may the preparations you are making in your heart bring you closer to your Savior. May you experience Him as your I Am today, and give Him thanks for all that He is, all that He has been, and all that He will be in your life.

December 15

LORD OF HOSTS

O come, all ye faithful,
Joyful and triumphant,
O come ye, O come ye to Bethlehem
Come and behold Him, born the King of angels.
O come, let us adore Him
O come, let us adore Him
O come, let us adore Him
Christ the Lord

Like the President of the United States, the Sovereign of the United Kingdom, King Charles, is head of the armed forces. For over 250 years over 1400 parading soldiers, 200 horses, and 400 musicians have come together for the recognition of the reigning monarch's birthday. It's a tradition called Trooping the Colors and is filled with great fun and fanfare. The soldiers show up in full battle dress, showing their readiness to serve and protect their commander-in-chief.

In Exodus 34, God described Himself to Moses as compassionate, gracious, slow to anger, abounding in love and faithfulness, maintaining love to thousands, and forgiving wickedness, rebellion, and sin. So when I was reading through the Old Testament, I was struck by the number of times God is referred to as Lord of Hosts. The angelic host is the angelic army. They are outfitted for battle. Elisha saw them riding horses with chariots of fire and said they greatly outnumbered their enemies. The Lord of Hosts commands His army and His enemies are defeated.

In Luke 2, when we are told that a heavenly host showed up the night Jesus was born this means a heavenly army accompanied Him from Heaven and made themselves visible to the shepherds. A frightful and powerful sight, no doubt. But I have to wonder, was this a Heavenly Trooping the Color on the birthday of their King? Or was this a matter of the angelic armies of Heaven accompanying their Commander in Chief on His redemptive mission, protecting Him from the enemy forces who no doubt were assembling their own army that night to threaten what they believed was this helpless Christ child?

But His enemies would not be getting near that infant King that night, because it was the multitude of the heavenly host—innumerable angel warriors, as far as the eye could see.

This Lord of Hosts, this King of Angels, is the God we serve. He is the One who will fight our battles. That struggle with sin? Those addictions that threaten your family? That pain? That financial setback that you can't overcome? It doesn't matter what the battle is—He will fight for you today. When you feel overpowered, too spiritually weak, already defeated, call out to the One who can, and will, protect you. Your enemy is His enemy, and He is the only one who can give you victory.

Glorify Him today as the Lord of Hosts. Worship His righteousness and holiness, and His power to defeat every enemy that comes against His purposes. Thank Him that the day is coming soon when the final enemy will be defeated, and we will live for eternity in His glorious kingdom in peace.

December 16

SON OF GOD, SON OF MAN

John 17:1-26

My friend, Angela, was adopted when she was an infant. She grew up the daughter of a Baptist minister and his lovely wife. But of course, through the years, she has wondered about her biological parents. I asked Angela to share her story for today's devotional, and with her typical grace, she agreed. Here are her words,

> *Growing up as an adopted only child, I often wondered about my biological parents and any possible siblings that could be out there in the world. It nagged at me at odd times. For example, I wondered if she thought of me every year on November 4th, my birthday.*

> *About ten years ago, I received some of the non-identifying information about my birth mother. She was seventeen, loved to read, and wore glasses. My birth father had no idea I even existed. That was unexpected. Cue forward about eight years; I decided to bite the proverbial bullet. I hired a professional company to search for my birth parents.*

> *My genealogist is well-known and very skilled. However, she has had no luck finding my birth mother. But she was able to find my birth father. Imagine my surprise when he was the absolute opposite of the father I grew up with. You see, my*

birth father looked as if he were straight out of central casting for "Sons of Anarchy." He even passed away while riding his motorcycle. He has five children (other than me), which gave me two sisters and three brothers.

I have heard wonderful and amazing things about him. He had green eyes (like me) and was a lover of animals (as am I). He was very outgoing, never met a stranger, and apparently would give anyone the shirt right off his back. All of those traits we share. He was so popular in his circle that they have a ride in his memory every year to commemorate him, which makes me smile.

My half-siblings are scattered from Georgia to Colorado and I hope one day to meet them.

As for my birth mother, that chapter of my life is still unwritten, but I hope one day my genealogist finds that elusive link that will answer all of my questions once and for all.

I am so excited about Angela's journey to discover her birth parents. I can imagine the emotion it brings to her when she finds these traits she has in common with them. It's that family resemblance, passed down through our DNA, that God knit together in our mothers' wombs.

When Jesus was born in Bethlehem, I have to imagine Mary gazing into his face, and like every mother does, trying to see even a glimmer of herself in Him. Mary knew He was the Son of God, she knew He was not Joseph's biological son. But did He have her nose? Her chin? Did He inherit those dimples from her? Was there the slightest hint in His countenance of what God Himself looks like? I wonder when we meet Mary in Heaven if we will see a family resemblance between her and Jesus.

Jesus, the Son of God, but also the Son of Man. This truth is one of the foundational doctrines of Christianity. But it's one that carries with it great mystery. Theological studies of the doctrine of the Sonship of Christ are intensely deep. Some of them can actually make my head spin. But I like how Dr. Tony Evans summarizes this in his book, *The Power of Jesus' Names*. He writes,

> *Jesus reveals the heart, goals, character, attributes, and desires of God to us. But He also identifies with our hearts, goals, character, attributes, and desires as humans....This is why He could be hungry one moment, but the next moment feed 5,000 people. He could be thirsty one moment, and the next moment walk on water. One moment He could die. Then, in another moment, He could rise from the dead.*

There is a beautiful connection between God the Father, God the Son (Jesus), and us. I John 3 declares,

> *Behold what love the Father has lavished on us, that we should be called children of God. And that is what we are!*

Because of Jesus' birth, death, and resurrection, those of us who have accepted His gift of faith have become co-heirs with Jesus, legally adopted children of God. In Galatians 4, Paul writes,

> *But when the fullness of the time came, God sent forth His Son, born of a woman, born under the Law, so that He might redeem those who were under the Law, that we might receive the adoption as sons.*

In other words, because He is the Son of God and the Son of Man, we can also be the children of God. Jesus has bridged the gap so that in our humanity, we can be made one with each other and with God. Because of His sacrificial work, we can accomplish the purpose He has for us and be partakers of the full measure of joy He offers.

John 17, the account of Christ's prayer in the Garden of Gethsemane before His arrest and death, is an intimate look at the relationship between God the Father and Christ the Son. Take a few moments to read this chapter in your Bible, and you'll be moved by the sweetness of the words in Jesus' prayer.

I can imagine John, who had been invited to eavesdrop on this moment between Father and Son, being overwhelmed with all he was hearing—at the time, not fully understanding it. But when the Holy Spirit allowed the memory of that conversation to flow from his pen, how he must have been breathless to think of the work of the cross in an even more beautiful light.

The heart of Jesus' prayer that night was this,

> *Father, the hour has come; glorify Your Son, that the Son may glorify You.*

The truth that God's Word tells us through John is that our redemption, though prompted by God's great love for us, was ultimately for His glory. And in His prayer for us, He didn't pray that we would be safe, healthy, and prosperous. He prayed that we would be sanctified that we would be unified, and that we would be kept in His name—His children—for His glory.

Being kept in His name means that we are kept—preserved for eternity—under the power and authority of God. Having His name attached to my very being gives me a great sense of peace and security because this means that the entire character and nature of God is intent upon keeping me for Himself. He has given me His name and made me His child. How can I even begin to fathom this relationship and all that it means?

Because He is my Father, I am to resemble Him. Because of my relationship with Christ, I should find myself becoming more and more like Him, and as a result, He will be glorified through me. Just like Mary looked for bits of herself in the Christ-child on that first Advent, I like to imagine Jesus looking for bits of Himself in me. No, I may not have His nose or His chin. But I can have His heart and His love, and a portion of His righteousness. As others see Him in me, He is glorified, and the Father is glorified, because the world knows that He has given me His name.

Today, glorify Him as the Son of God and Son of Man. Can you see a family resemblance in your own life? Can Jesus see Himself in you?

December 17

THE WAY

Isaiah 35:8-10; John 14:1-6

Bruce Olson was a missionary to the Motilone tribe in Colombia. His heart for these Indians was so strong, he left his home in the United States at age 19. He had no college education and no backing from any mission group. After living with a group of Motilones in their communal home for five years, he was finally given his first chance to tell them about Jesus. The Motilones had a desire to know God, and they had a distinct and deep sense of their lostness. Their ancestors had been deceived before and had followed false teachers who led them astray. And now they were lost. But they were also quick to dismiss, sometimes to the point of death, those who threatened their traditions and way of life.

One day while walking the jungle trails, Bruce and his companions heard two men crying loudly. This was unusual because the Motilones normally showed no emotion such as sorrow. Bruce turned aside to see what was wrong with the two men. One was wailing into the sky and one into a hole in the ground. They were trying to find God.

Bruce told them about Jesus, and how He was the One to lead them to God. He explained to them how Jesus is God's Son, and how He came down from Heaven to be like us so that He could show us the way. In his autobiography, Olson writes,

They gasped. There was a tense, hushed silence. The idea that God had become a man stunned them.

"Where did He walk?" the witch doctor asked in a whisper.

Every Motilone has his own trail. It is his personal point of identity. You walk on someone's trail if you want to find him. God would have a trail, too. If you want to find God, you walk on His trail.

"Jesus Christ is God become man," I said. "He can show you God's trail."

In the upper room, before He left them for the cross, Jesus was preparing His disciples for His departure. What would they do without Him? Perhaps they were already feeling a little lost as well as confused. But He assured them they already knew the way to get to Him. Thomas, the doubter, questioned Him, but again Jesus assured him by saying,

I am the way.

There was no esoteric meaning behind this—the word used there for *"way"* literally means "the way to go." It was used many times in the New Testament. Jesus is the way to go to Heaven because He secured our redemption. But the sweetest part about the whole conversation is that Jesus wasn't just telling His disciples how to get to Heaven—He was telling them how they could get to Him,

That where I am, there you also may be.

Jesus wants us to find His way. Since man's first sin in the Garden of Eden, God has been making a way for us back to Him. And He has been marking that path, making it so very clear—all we need is faith, and in His graciousness, He even gives us that as His gift.

In Matthew 7, the Sermon on the Mount, Jesus tells the crowd to *enter through the narrow gate; for the gate is wide and the way is broad that leads to destruction, and there are many who enter through it. For the gate is small and the way is narrow that leads to life, and there are few who find it.*

The world's way is so much easier to see, isn't it? It's marked by bright and shiny things, warm and soft things. It's marked by power, position, and possessions. Like kittens distracted by the red laser light, we chase things that we'll never catch—or if we somehow do, we find they can never be enough, they can never resolve that feeling of lostness. Even when those things are good works that we do—feeding the hungry, or volunteering at a homeless shelter—when we do those things as a means to save ourselves, we will find ourselves just as lost as before. Lost, tired, and spent.

During Advent, we remember how God guided the wise men, the Magi, to Christ. We remember the star that led them hundreds of miles. And what an amazing, precise journey that was. But we often forget that this journey required those Magi to search. They first went to Jerusalem asking where they could find the King of the Jews. Even though they knew the prophecy of the star, they needed someone to tell them from Scripture the exact place He was. Ironically, though the Jewish scholars knew the answer to the Magis' question, they had no desire to search for their promised King.

The Magi had to keep their minds and their eyes focused on their goal— to see the Messiah and to worship Him. And we have to do that as well because sometimes it's easy to get distracted and off-track. It's so very tempting to take our eyes off of Jesus and put them on the world. Once we are on the narrow way, once we belong to Him, we won't ever be lost again. But to live in the victory we are meant to enjoy, we do need to keep our eyes on Him. To continue to follow Him, we need to walk His trail.

Paul exhorts us in the New Testament that we are to walk in a new way than we did before we became believers. In Ephesians 5 he tells us that we are to be

> *imitators of God, as beloved children; and walk in love, just as Christ also loved you and gave Himself up for us, an offering and a sacrifice to God as a fragrant aroma.*

How precious this encouragement is to follow Him as His children who are dearly loved.

Sometimes, it can be difficult. This world doesn't make it easy to follow Christ, and we can grow weary and wonder if we'll ever make it. There is a passage in Isaiah 35 that always encourages me when the narrow way gets challenging. The prophet tells us about the Highway of Holiness. There will neither be anyone nor anything on that road that will tempt us to sin. It will be a road for the redeemed only, the ransomed of the Lord. It is the road that will lead us to our everlasting joy in Heaven, where there will be only gladness and joy, and sorrow and sighing will flee away.

The promises and hope we have of eternal life grow sweeter every day of this journey we are on toward Christ's second Advent. As you think about Jesus today, thank Him for being the Way. Thank Him for making that narrow path so clear, thank Him for the grace He gives you each day to stay true and faithful. And thank Him, most of all, that His way leads us directly to Him.

How would your life be different if today you glorified Him as The Way?

December 18

THE TRUTH

Psalm 89:14; John 1:17

(*Parents Proceed with Caution*)

I was meandering around Amazon doing some early Christmas shopping and I came across something interesting. Evidently, parents can purchase kits of items that, properly used, will encourage their children to continue to believe in Santa. Items you can order are buttons from Santa's coat, a magic key he uses to get into homes without chimneys, floor stencils of boot prints, and even a shoe from a reindeer hoof.

No matter how long parents work to keep the magic of Santa returning on Christmas mornings, eventually, the kids are going to figure it out. Recently I conducted an informal poll of friends and family members about how they found out the truth about Santa. While there were those whose friends at school or whose family members dropped the truth on them, many of them just figured it out.

As my husband told me, "I just realized it one day. I thought, 'This can't be real.'" It just no longer made any sense to him. He was about eight years old at the time, and he went to his mother and informed her that he was aware of the truth. And, he said, if Santa isn't real, then obviously that means the Tooth Fairy and Easter Bunny can't be real either. "Well," his mom said, "I guess you've got it all figured out then." And that was the end of the matter.

In her book, *Live Your Truth and Other Lies*, Alisa Childers relates the story of her young daughter, who had sorted out the truth about magical and mythical creatures at a young age, coming home one day from preschool to announce that "Lepwechauns are weal." The child's teacher, in what social media would call "cuteness overload," planted "evidence" that a real-life leprechaun had decorated the classroom for Saint Patrick's Day. Her daughter's impressionable mind, though formerly made up about this matter, was now persuaded otherwise.

In John 14, Jesus reminded His disciples that He is the Truth. Truth is a word that refers to a foundational reality. The truth is true regardless of opinion. What is true will remain true no matter if everything else around it changes. And what is true is universally true no matter how hard and loud the world will tell us that truth is personal. Jesus Himself was the embodiment of the truth of God's promise to send a Messiah, a Savior. He was, and is, the foundational reality of everything that is. He is our assurance, our certainty.

But, oh, how our culture tries to lull us into believing that truth is based on our personal thoughts and opinions. Culture tells us to listen to our hearts, to go with our emotions, our "feels," and our "vibes." Dangerously, social media will often pepper these thoughts about the relativism of truth with Scripture and misquotes from respected Biblical teachers. At this point, it may be important for us to remember, particularly in these days of 24-hour news and social media, that the one who is behind all of this manipulation, who has been behind it for ages, is Satan—the enemy of our souls. He is the prince of the power of the air, so we should take great care of all that we hear and read through the media.

If we are inundated with falsehoods and if we are bombarded with instructions to live our own truths, find ourselves, and follow our hearts—how do we sort this all out? How do we know Jesus as the one Who is The Truth?

The obvious answer is that we should immerse ourselves in the Word of God. Some people find this answer to be trite and find the Bible to be intimidating. They find it hard to read and understand. Some people are just plain afraid of it. I would like to suggest that these personal fears and opinions are, again, fed by the enemy, and the harder you feel it is to read the Bible, the harder you need to press into it—because there is something there that God needs to communicate to you.

If you are a believer in Christ, you have been given the gift of His presence—the Holy Spirit—in your life. Jesus calls Him the Spirit of Truth, and He is the one who will guide us into all truth, He is the One who will disclose all truth to us. If reading Scripture is new or hard to you, you do not need to be afraid to open that Bible—God's got you covered. He will make sure you hear from Him.

Jesus told us that we would know we are truly His disciples if we remain in His Word. He said in John 8, that when we do remain in His word,

You will know the truth and the truth will make you free.

How do we know, you may ask, when we've heard from Him? How do we know when it's God who is speaking to us? In my life, it's just like my husband explained about his experience with Santa—it's just a sudden realization. Something that before was fuzzy to you, or something that you had wrongly believed was right, is suddenly clear. You just know—not in your heart or emotions, but in the spiritual part of you that will live forever, a certainty is reached, and you know that you have just experienced Jesus—the Truth. His presence and His work in our lives are unmistakable.

Man has been seeking the truth since his banishment from God's presence in the Garden of Eden, and this is the case more so today than ever. To fulfill His promise, and to bring us face to face with the Truth Himself, God sent Jesus to earth. In His human form, He was the embodiment of all that God is. As the Truth, Jesus is the absolute certainty, He is our unshaken assurance of the faithfulness of God. We can respond to all that the world throws at us in utter confidence that we are kept, we are set apart, sanctified, in His truth. This was the prayer Jesus prayed for us, and no prayer He ever asked of His Father went unanswered.

Today be assured that Jesus is the only Truth. In times of uncertainty, in times of confusion, reach out to Him. Thank Him for His presence in your life that keeps you set apart and hidden from all the lies of the enemy. During this time of Advent, ask Him to give you the gift of a fresh love for His Word, and a desire to remain in His Word, so that you can know the Truth that will make you free.

December 19

THE LIFE

John 1:1-4

When I was six years old, I was a young mother to several dolls that were spoiled and pampered, but still very well-behaved for the most part. Dolls were interesting creatures in my childhood. They were made of rubber or some form of plastic, which made them perfect for real-world baby situations like bath time and diaper changes. Their heads popped off so after their bath they could be drained of any water and/or bubbles. Sometimes arms and legs popped off, too. Those weren't as easy to reattach. Most likely every little girl's toybox contained a frightening menagerie of extra limbs from dolls long abandoned.

Of course, every doll needed to be fed, and of special interest and curiosity to me were the bottles that came with magic milk. That was the milk that seemed to disappear as you fed your doll. After the doll was fed and the bottle placed upright, the milk would reappear. Magic!

Then one day it was 1973 and a toy company introduced a new kind of doll. It was called Baby Alive, and I wanted one! When you pushed on the doll's chin, she would suck a real bottle! She would even eat "real" food, mixed with packets of some sort of powder and real water! Of course, this type of situation required actual diaper changes, and not to worry—Baby Alive came with real diapers!

Oh, how I wished and prayed for that Baby Alive doll. Every Christmas and every birthday came and went, and even when I was well over the age when I played with dolls, there was a little part of me that was slightly put out that the one thing I really wanted was something I didn't get. Then in my late 30s, after sharing this story with a ladies' Sunday school class, a mysterious package showed up, with a note from "Santa" explaining that the doll had been lost all that time, but "he" was happy to finally deliver it to me.

Well, that Baby Alive doll was no more alive than the other dolls I played with. It was just soft plastic with a mechanical device that made its mouth move. The doll couldn't experience hunger, love, or sadness. It was just a composite of inanimate parts through which no life breath flowed.

It has always somewhat amazed me that the God who could speak plants and animals into being, with a life force specific to their species, chose to get His hands dirty to make man. He formed man from the dust, breathing His own breath into the man's lungs. And He fashioned woman from man. We were created in a very special way for a very special purpose—for a very special life. That life was one of abundance and joy, of peace and fellowship, of fulfillment in the tasks God had ordained man to do and in the relationships He intended man to have.

We know what happened, don't we? Sin happened. And all that was meant to be was swallowed up in that first bite of the single fruit God had said, "No" to. Everything else in that lush garden was thumbs up for man. It was good for food, so it satisfied man physically. It was pleasing to the sight, so it satisfied man emotionally. The knowledge and life stored in those two trees were not off limits, the fruit was. God always intended man to come directly to Him for the knowledge and the life the two trees offered. But Satan zeroed in on those things and man fell for it.

What was true in the garden is still true for us today. Physically we have breath in our lungs and blood flowing through our veins and arteries. We experience emotions, pain, hunger, thirst—everything humans were created to experience. But to have the true life of abundance and fulfillment we were meant to have we must receive it from God.

Jesus, God Incarnate, came to give us the life that only He can give. Man has been trying for thousands of years to find fulfillment, true fulfillment. Man has crafted millions of little-g gods and idols, knowing that abundance doesn't come from himself, yet always seeking it.

I'm reminded of the Apostle Paul preaching in Athens. He noted all the statues and shrines to gods covering every aspect of life on earth. But there was another shrine there as well—the shrine to the unknown god. They knew something was missing. Paul explained to them who that God is. He is, Paul said, the God in whom

we live and move and exist.

Jesus is the life we are looking for. According to my Greek Lexicon, the term "life" as used in John 14:6, was used to specify genuine life. Jesus was referring to an active life, that was happy and blessed here on earth, but one that would be even more fulfilling in eternity. Jesus also promised that He had come to the earth so that we could not only have life but have that fulfilling life in abundance. Completely fulfilled, never sensing lack, never a wavering of joy or peace. How could that be?

I think Paul's instruction to us to keep our minds set on things above, and not on things on the earth is the key. This is in Colossians 3 and he writes,

For you have died and your life is hidden with Christ in God. When Christ, who is our life, is revealed, then you will also be revealed with Him in glory.

Wait, I'm not dead yet. What could it mean that I have died? Paul goes on to explain, *consider the members of your earthly body as dead to immorality, impurity, passion, evil desire, and greed, which amounts to idolatry.*

As you read that list, you may be thinking, "I'm a good person, and I don't do any of those things, but I still don't *feel* abundant life." It's not just what we *don't do* that makes us a good steward of the life Jesus has brought us. Later on, Paul tells us that the new life we have been given by Christ should be marked with *compassion, kindness, gentleness, and patience, bearing with one another, and forgiving each other....* He goes on to say we are to let the peace of Christ reign in our hearts—by letting go of things that bring strife. We are to be thankful. We are to let the word of Christ dwell in our mouths. In other words, when people see us—they should see a clear reflection of Him. They should see His glory.

Remember, our very purpose is to reflect the glory of God. Every bit of our being is to glorify Him. As we draw closer to that second Advent we are waiting for right now, it's ever more important that we are careful to draw the eyes of everyone who sees us to our Savior. The life you have today may be filled with hardship. You may be experiencing sickness, loss, loneliness, or financial hardship. No matter what He has allowed, let your life honor Him knowing even in this abundance can be found because Jesus is your life.

December 20

REDEEMER

Isaiah 43:1-3

Ralphie Parker, protagonist in the holiday favorite movie, *A Christmas Story*, worked hard for that Little Orphan Annie Speed-O-Matic Secret Decoder Pin. For weeks he had to drink gallons of Ovaltine, then send in the inner seal, and now, pin in hand, he was ready to decode the secret message the announcer called out at the end of the Little Orphan Annie radio program.

With studied precision, listening as carefully as any nine-year-old boy could listen, Ralphie carefully wrote down the numbers, then headed straight to the only room in the house where a boy of nine could sit in privacy and decode. As mom and little brother Randy banged on the bathroom door, Ralphie diligently, with sweat glistening on his brow, decoded the message.

As the banging on the door and the shouting for him to hurry, intensified, Ralphie continued to work. His fingers flew! His mind was a steel trap! Every pore vibrated! Finally, the secret message was fully revealed to him. "Be sure to drink your Ovaltine." Yes, it was a crummy commercial. As Ralphie exited the bathroom, he went out to face the world again. Wiser.

Ovaltine's Little Orphan Annie Decoder Pin label redemption program is just one example of a marketing plan that encourages consumers to keep purchasing a particular item from a particular brand. Buy enough of a product, redeem a certain amount of labels, and get "a prize." It's a way for businesses to, essentially, buy their customer's loyalty.

The concept of redemption in Scripture carries a much heavier weight than this. Today, let's think about two things that Christ as our Redeemer means for us. First, redemption is a transactional act. Adam and Eve sinned, and in a way, they unwittingly sold themselves to the enemy of their souls. In that moment, they chose to place themselves under the authority of Satan, and this singular act brought eternal consequences for all mankind.

But God has a great love for us. In Exodus 34, God described Himself to Moses,

> *The Lord, the Lord God, compassionate and gracious, slow to anger, and abounding in lovingkindness and truth; who keeps lovingkindness for thousands, who forgives iniquity, transgression, and sin; yet He will by no means leave the guilty unpunished.*

He wanted us back. But all of mankind was guilty and required punishment—that punishment came with a heavy price tag, a perfect sacrifice. No mortal man would be able to pay the price of man's redemption. No mortal man could be perfect. So God overcame this constraint by sending His perfect Son Jesus, the Incarnate God, to pay the price—death—for our lives. In that act, He bought us back from Satan.

There was another aspect of the Redeemer in Scripture, and that was the aspect of the Kinsman Redeemer. When a man died leaving a wife and property, his closest relative had the responsibility of marrying the widow and purchasing his property. This was an arrangement that helped provide for families who were left without an heir after the death of the husband. There were three things involved—the Kinsman Redeemer had to be a close relative, he had to be willing to be the redeemer, and he had to be able to be the redeemer.

For the redemption of mankind, only Jesus could meet all three conditions. He was able to be our Kinsman Redeemer because He was the sinless Lamb of God. He was willing to Redeem us because of His great love and mercy for us. And in coming to Earth in human flesh, He was our close relative.

This idea of redemption may sound a little heavy and perhaps even sorrowful, but in reality, it was a matter of great celebration. It was the offering of hope for those in a hopeless situation. It was the provision of help for those who were helpless. It was the assigning of a name to those who were left struggling to find a new identity after a devastating loss. Even with all of this, our redemption had a more important purpose, and that was God's own glory.

Through the prophet Isaiah, God told Israel,

> *But now, this says the Lord, your Creator, O Jacob, and He who formed you O Israel, Do not fear, for have redeemed you; I have called you by name; you are Mine.*

He created us. He formed us. He bought us back from the power of Satan. He made us His own. But it's so important that we don't lose sight of His "why," and that goes back to His ultimate purpose for all of Creation—the glory of His name. It is His name that brings beauty, majesty, and holiness into this world. If we are to have purity of joy, love, peace, and hope, it is going to be as we witness and participate in the glory of His name.

Today, His name is Redeemer. Worship Him for the great sacrifice that made us His own. Give Him thanks for His willingness to pay the price to buy us back and make us free from the bondage of sin. Give Him praise for your redemption, purchased by His blood, that makes you His child for all eternity. As you continue to look toward Advent, may your faith grow ever stronger, and may your joy abound. His name is Redeemer, and you are His redeemed.

December 21

MESSIAH

John 4:25-30, 39

I once heard someone say that we are all the sum total of all the broken promises we've experienced in our lives. I'm not sure that's truly an accurate portrayal, but I do know that all of us have experienced our fair share of broken promises. And if we're completely honest, some of us have even been the promise-breakers.

When I consider the woman at the well in John 4, I think she was a woman who had experienced many broken promises in her life. She came to the well alone, wishing to remain anonymous, perhaps, but we can only deduce from the little we know about her—and that comes from the revelation of Jesus' conversation with her.

The climax of their conversation was not that he knew her life of multiple marriages and immoral relationships. She knew that almost everyone in town knew that. The climax was when she mentioned the matter of the Messiah, the Christ, that God had promised through the prophets would come—and Jesus declared to her, "I am He.

The name Messiah, which is most often translated as Christ in the New Testament, means "anointed one." He was the one God promised would come, anointed by God, to be the King and High Priest, who would redeem His people and rule over His creation. He would answer all their questions, and fulfill all their longings—and this woman, who had been experiencing broken promises for what seems like most of her adult life, was face to face with this promised Messiah.

Look at the faith she expresses in that statement—"*I **know** that Messiah is coming.*" It wasn't just hearsay to her—she trusted. It was her hope, in the middle of all her uncertainty from life's circumstances. She clung to that hope. In a very real sense, her faith was made sight. He had not come to a palace, He had come to her—that well she visited in the heat of the day, the picture of her loneliness.

I take great comfort in the fact that it was this woman Jesus chose to reveal His Messiahship to. She was a Samaritan, and the Samaritans and Jews were naturally at odds with one another. She was an outcast, having been married five times, but not married to the man she was currently living with. In those days, men could divorce women for the most innocent of offenses so we can understand the shame this woman must have carried around with her, but also her loneliness, confusion, and distrust. All those broken promises probably made her somewhat guarded, particularly in a conversation with a Jewish man.

But something in how He gently spoke to her, in the way He so kindly pointed out the thing that was wrong in her life and offered Himself as the answer she was looking for, He broke through all her shame and confusion. He was her hope and she knew it as certainty because He spoke with the authority of the Anointed One, the Messiah. There was no question in her mind that He was truly the One they had all been waiting for.

The Christmas season is a time when many people feel the weight of all the broken relationships and the broken promises in their lives. There's a heaviness in the hearts of many people that seems even heavier as the world is wrapped up in festive decorations, music, laughter, and friendship. Shame and confusion can make the joy of the season seem somehow ominous and hard to bear. Some seek solitude to hide the hurt they feel, and to cover their loneliness. Others try to mask their broken hearts with frivolity and superficial celebrations, with volunteering and donating and gifting beyond their means. All of these things are just the desert well at midday.

On the day that Jesus met the woman at the well, somewhere in the world there was political unrest. Somewhere battles were being fought. Somewhere crimes were being committed by cruel and wicked people. But that day Jesus stopped by the well to get personal with a Samaritan woman. It was her world of shame and loneliness and fear that He entered that day. It was to this woman He first revealed Himself as the Messiah— the Anointed One, the Promised One. Her King.

One day, the Messiah will return to this earth as a conquering, victorious King, overtaking all the evil in the world, abolishing the wicked kingdom of Satan, and establishing God's kingdom of righteousness. We long for that day—we long to see the beauty of His holiness, and to serve Him, worship Him, and glorify Him for all eternity in our Heavenly home.

But today, He wants to enter into your world in a personal way. He wants to lovingly point out those things in your life that He came to overcome— the shame, the shortcomings—everything that is wrong, He wants to show you how He can make it right. He will come into your aloneness, at your midday well, ready to reveal Himself to you just as He did that Samaritan woman.

He is your Messiah. Glorify Him today by letting Him change you. Open up your heart, confess those things that are shameful to you, and allow Him to look into your eyes and speak into your midday well moment. Then leave that place with joy and gladness, free from those burdensome things you've carried too long.

This Advent, as you are reminded of His birth, life, death, and resurrection, don't forget that there is still a promise on the table—the promise of His long-awaited, and imminent, return.

December 22

SOON COMING KING

Let every heart prepare Him room
And heaven and nature sing!

The words to the beloved Christmas carol, "Joy to the World," were written by Isaac Watts. As a young man, he noticed the lack of interest on the faces of the people in church as they sang the worship songs. The lyrics to this carol, based on Psalm 98, were meant to create a sense of joy. But the song wasn't really about the birth of Jesus—it is specifically about His second Advent.

The coming of our Lord Jesus, of our King, should be an unshakeable source of joy for us. Knowing that one day our Creator, our Redeemer, and the Lover of our souls will be with us should pierce through the daily grind of life. Thoughts of eternity with Him in a place where no sin or wickedness can ever enter should give us peace when the world is at war. It should give us comfort during days of great fear and uncertainty.

He is coming for us, and the day of His appearance is closer than it's ever been. He is our soon-coming King. Do our faces and our lives reflect the joy we feel when we consider it? What about how we spend our money? Our time? How we conduct ourselves with unbelievers—especially with unbelieving family members? Are we living lives of conviction and love?

Advent is a time for our hearts to prepare room for Him. How would your life be different today if you were to fully glorify Him as your soon-coming King?

December 23

LAMB OF GOD

John 1:29-30, 35-37

No Christmas pageant is complete without the lamb. The lamb is endearing and lovable. It's fluffy and soft. Who can resist a sweet rosy-cheeked toddler, crowned with a set of felt ears and cotton puff tail, hair curled to resemble the snowy fleece of a little Christmas lamb?

It was December of 2017 in White Pines, Tennessee, and the preschoolers at First Baptist Church were eager to get up on stage and dance to the Christmas music during the church's nativity program. Teegan Benson, just two years old at the time, was all decked out as the nativity lamb. But all during rehearsals, Teegan had been plotting. She really wanted that doll in the manger. She had been talking about it to her mom for weeks—she intended to get that baby Jesus in her hands.

And that is what she did. Midway through "Away in a Manger," little Teegan, with her curls and fluffy white sheep costume, grabbed up baby Jesus and began rocking him as the children sang. The baby's "mother," three-year-old "Mary," promptly rescued the doll-child from the sheep and plopped him right back in the manger. Teegan, not to be outdone, grabbed the baby again. The altercation ended with Mary putting the fluffy little lamb in a headlock.

When John the Baptist introduced Jesus, it was this name, Lamb of God, to which he referred,

Behold, the Lamb of God who takes away the sin of the world!" (John 1:9)

Earlier in the chapter we're told that the Pharisees had sent priests and Levites to learn from John what he was preaching about and what kind of baptism he was performing. So when John referred to Jesus as the Lamb of God who takes away the sin of the world, this was a powerful image for his audience, most likely reminding them of the Passover Lamb, and possibly even taking them back to Abraham and Isaac. To these priests and Levites, this would have been a shocking title. Let's think about what these men knew about sacrificial lambs and what this means to us.

Twice every day a lamb was sacrificed at the Temple in Jerusalem. In fact, with Bethlehem's proximity to Jerusalem, it's thought that perhaps the shepherds who were the first to hear of the birth of Jesus were tending lambs that were being raised for Temple sacrifices. These lambs had to be unblemished to be fit for the Temple. But no matter how perfect these lambs were, and no matter how perfectly the priests carried out the ritual sacrifices, the spilling of their blood only provided limited atonement.

Animal sacrifice could never provide full payment for man's sin because it was not an equal sacrifice—a lamb was an animal, and the life of an animal could never equal the value of a man's soul.

But no mere man could ever atone for his own sin, either, because man can't meet the standard God requires—the standard of perfect holiness. Sometimes I fear this concept of perfect holiness is lost on us. We live in a world that desires tolerance of anything a sinful man can imagine. Some use the accounts of Jesus eating with sinners as evidence that He would approve of godless men and women, and therefore so should the church. False teaching such as this is rampant during these days so we must take care to remember that while Christ sought out sinners, it was not in approval of their sin—it was to extend the kindness and mercy of God that lovingly draws us to repentance from those sins.

Also, Jesus never redefined sin. In our day, it's the norm for couples to live together and begin having children before marriage is even mentioned. I've had many conversations with Christians about their view of this, and almost across the board their opinion is, "It doesn't matter." It matters to God, though. Dr. Tony Evans says,

> *God only accepts what He accepts. He doesn't accept what you want Him to accept just because it's acceptable to you. Have you ever had someone do some work on your house, and they thought they did a good job, but you had to tell them you weren't satisfied with what they did? The reason why your viewpoint matters is because you are the owner of the house. Similarly, God's standard is what matters when it comes to His creation. He will accept nothing less than perfection.*

No, Jesus never waived the requirement for perfect holiness—He fulfilled it by becoming our perfect substitute.

One of the most significant sacrifices for the Jewish people was the paschal, or Passover, lamb. This was the lamb that was offered in obedience and remembrance for God's delivering the people of Israel from Egypt. This point in Israel's history is the perfect picture of redemption—of God "buying back" His people from their enemy. This was a picture that God never wanted His people to forget—so He instructed them to open each year with a celebration to mark His work of redemption.

This Passover celebration was not just a remembrance for His people—it was meant to build their anticipation for the time when the Messiah, the Lamb of God, would come. This Lamb, God's Son, Jesus, would be the one to provide perfect atonement for all who will believe in Him because He would be the perfect sacrifice. Paul referenced this in I Corinthians 5:7 when he wrote,

For Christ, our Passover also has been sacrificed.

John's words not only pointed to Jesus as God's perfect Lamb, but he also declared that this Lamb would serve as a sacrifice for both the Jew and the Gentile. It was perhaps the first time the priests and Levites really faced the fact that the only true God they served was not just the God of the Jews but was the God of all who would place their faith in Jesus—whether Jew or Gentile. This redemption would cross borders never before imagined and would be offered to people all over the world.

Once Christ gave His life on Calvary, no longer would those daily sacrifices be required. He paid in full the penalty for the sins of all the world. It was a costly redemption. Peter reminds us that we

> *were not redeemed with perishable things like silver or gold from your futile way of life inherited from your forefathers* (referring here to the system of animal sacrifice), *but with precious blood, as of a lamb unblemished and spotless, the blood of Christ.* (I Peter 1:18-19)

I wonder how many of us still agonize and strive in a futile way of trying to redeem ourselves. How many of us try to justify ourselves, living lives filled with guilt we try to hide, and thinking we can replace a sinful deed or thought with a "good" deed or thought and somehow make ourselves appealing to God? It just doesn't work that way, and thank God, it doesn't. Thank God He has provided a way to be redeemed through the act of simple faith in what the Lamb of God has done.

In Revelation 5 we find a beautiful picture of the glory of this name. In this passage, John sees in his heavenly vision a book with seven seals that no one is worthy to open. It was a thought that caused him to weep—until he saw

> *a Lamb standing, as if slain.... And He came and took the book out of the right hand of Him who sat on the throne. When He had taken the book, the four living creatures, and the*

twenty-four elders fell down before the Lamb....And they sang a new song, saying, "Worthy are You to take the book and to break its seals; for You were slain, and purchased for God with Your blood men from every tribe and tongue and people and nation. You have made them to be a kingdom and priests to our God, and they will reign upon the earth."
(Revelation 5:6-10)

As you consider this today, give Him thanks and praise for your salvation, for your redemption. If you find yourself still trying to be acceptable to God, stop for a moment—confess that you are not able to meet His standard of perfect holiness, thank Him for the sacrifice of His Son, and ask Him for the grace and the faith to trust Him as your perfect Lamb. This Lamb of God has taken away my sins and your sins. Not just for a day, but for all eternity. That perfect blood He shed was enough—it was all we could ever need. He alone is worthy. Worship Him for this today.

December 24

BRIDEGROOM

Matthew 25:1-13

In May of 1989, I received a special college graduation gift—a hand-made quilt, large enough for a full-sized bed—from my great-aunt Elsie Blackmore, a woman I had never personally met, but who thought enough of me to send me such a special gift. The thing is, these were the days of mauve, dusty rose, and country blue. We were into soft peaches and greens, or burgundies and navies. But the quilt was a patchwork of lovingly placed squares of orange gingham, brown gingham, and white. I packed it carefully in a Rubbermaid container and stored it away. Over the years I've taken it out and considered using it, but I've just never had a place for an orange and brown quilt.

In May of this year, 2024, at age 57, I married for the first time. Of course, since the days I was a young woman I've wanted a husband and family, but those prayers always went unanswered. So, over the years, I just gradually decided to embrace the life God had clearly chosen for me. I learned to love my single life. I had a nice home, some cats, a yard to plant flowers in, and a great church family. I was content. Until last summer.

One evening I was listening to an audiobook when the Lord tapped me on the shoulder and said, "You need 'a friend.' Start praying for one."

Without considering it, I said, "No. I'm not going to pray for that. I'm happy. Why do I want to start getting my hopes up only to be disappointed? Please give me another prayer."

He didn't listen. God's funny that way, isn't He?

"Okay," I finally said. "I'll pray for 'a friend'. But I'm going to have some conditions. I will not go looking on the internet for said 'friend,' so You're going to have to bring him to me where I am. This means either work or church. Oh, and I'm not going to date anyone from work. That leaves the church." This was a perfect strategy, I thought, since I knew there were no single men at my church.

"Furthermore," I told Him, "I'm not walking into church every week scanning the pews for a single man. That means you'll need to plop him down in the pew beside me. You know exactly where I sit so that shouldn't be hard." Oh, the attitude I had! Praying a prayer He had given me, but making it impossible for Him to answer. After all, I had 57 years of evidence that it was impossible. It was at that point that God reminded me of the verse,

Nothing shall be impossible with God.

In just a couple of months, a lady at my church sat down beside me at a baby shower and said, "I have someone I want you to meet."

The next morning she marched Mike Smith across the church and made introductions. Then she fled. Mike and I made small talk for about 5 minutes, until I said, "The prelude music is starting. You should go back to your seat." Oh, yes… I did, and we still laugh about that.

Mike walked away and I thought, "Well, that took care of that."

Until the next Sunday. Mike approached my pew and very politely asked, "May I sit with you?" I can't be certain, but I'm pretty sure I heard God chuckle. I heard a full-on belly laugh from Heaven when eight months later Mike was walking me up that same church aisle as his newly pronounced wife. I have to say, a good husband is definitely worth waiting for.

Before our wedding, Mike and I were down in the shed at my mom's house as I was preparing to move some things over to his house. I opened a Rubbermaid container to reveal a 35-year-old orange and brown gingham handmade quilt, in pristine condition. Mike loved it, and that quilt is now the centerpiece of our guest room—the perfect place for it.

On multiple occasions, Jesus is referred to as the Bridegroom. It is a picture of the beautiful love relationship He has with His bride, the church. In John 14, when Jesus tells His disciples that he is going to prepare a place for them, and speaks of His Father's house, He is painting a picture of a betrothed man, who leaves His bride for some time while He returns to His Father's home to prepare a room for H and His bride to live. When the room is ready, He will return for her and take her to her new home—just as one day, Christ will return for His bride to take us to our new home in Heaven.

In Matthew 25, Jesus tells a parable that describes what our business should be while we wait for His return. We are to be preparing ourselves by keeping "oil in our lamps." This is the parable of the ten virgins. Ten were wise and kept their lamps filled with oil so that when they heard of the bridegroom's arriving, they would be ready to go and meet him. It was the custom during those days that when a bridegroom returned for his bride, he would arrive at night—so a betrothed woman needed to keep her lamp ready.

Ten virgins had lamps, but only five had lamps filled with oil—only five had lamps that actually worked. The foolish virgins had lamps, but they didn't take seriously their responsibility to fill the lamp with that which made the lamp work for the purpose it was made. In Scripture, oil is a picture of the Holy Spirit, so it's safe to assume that the five virgins with no oil were without the Holy Spirit, in other words, they looked like they belonged to the bridegroom on the outside, but on the inside, they didn't have the faith that was required from of a true bride.

Advent is the time we prepare for our Bridegroom to return. As we adorn our trees with lights and our windows with candles, let's remember to keep our lamps filled with oil and our lives filled with Jesus. Though He may be delayed, He is coming for us, and one day, or one midnight, soon, we will hear His shout.

The orange and brown gingham quilt in my guest room is 35 years old, but it looks brand new. When I look at that quilt, I understand that during all the years I thought God had forgotten about me, He had not. He was preparing every detail of the home I now share with my husband. So just imagine the details He is preparing for our eternal home. When our Bridegroom appears and ushers us into His eternal Kingdom, this time of waiting will seem like the blink of an eye.

As He is preparing for me, I must be preparing for Him. Ask Him today to fill your lamp with the oil of His Spirit. As you glorify His name, *Bridegroom,* today, be filled with joy in knowing we will soon hear His voice calling us to the home He's prepared for us.

December 25

JESUS

Jesus. The One who makes this day holy and sets it apart. Not just a holiday to enjoy gifts, special meals, and traditions with family and friends. More than any other day of the year, today we can glorify this name, Jesus, with all joy and reverence.

Jesus. His name is the only name that brings redemption—the name that the Apostle Peter preached about when he said "There is no other name under heaven by which men can be saved," and the name the Apostle Paul was talking about when he said, "whoever calls on the name of the Lord will be saved."

His name is the name that brings us comfort when we feel alone in our suffering and struggles as we call out to Him, our Immanuel, the one Who is always with us. His name is the name that brings us confidence and victory when our battles exceed our strength. His name is the name that brings us peace when the whole world is at war.

It is the name that the world profanes, belittles, and blasphemes. For some, it is seen as a type of incantation—a magic word that brings about victory and prosperity.

But it's the name that one day will send every knee to the ground as every tongue confesses that He is Lord to the glory of God.

Today we celebrate by glorifying His name from what seems a great distance. But one day, His second Advent will be upon us, and we can glorify Him face to face for all eternity. That day is coming soon. Are you ready?

NOTES

It is never my intention to present the words or ideas of others as my own. Many pastors, teachers, and authors have influenced me, and I have attempted to credit everyone I've read or heard throughout my preparation and writing of this book in the notes below. Any failure to do so is purely unintentional.

I am indebted to the following commentaries which provided insight during my period of Scripture research and study:

Henry, Matthew. *Matthew Henry's Concise Commentary on the Whole Bible.* Thomas Nelson Publishers: Nashville. 1997.

MacArthur, John. The MacArthur Study Bible. New American Standard Bible. Updated Edition. Nelson Bibles. 2006.

Rydelnik, Michael and Vanlaningham, Michael ed. *The Moody Bible Commentary.* Moody Publishers: Chicago. 2014.

KEY OF DAVID

Gant, Andrew. *The Carols of Christmas.* Nelson Publishers: Nashville, TN. 2015

HALLOWED

Adewoye, Dayo. "Recovering Reverence." July 18, 2021. https://thechristianmindng.org/2021/07/18/recovering-reverence/.

Pettrey, Brian. "Our Father, Loving & Powerful." Sermon delivered at Brooklyn Tabernacle, Brooklyn, NY. June 26, 2024.

ALPHA AND OMEGA

Cook, Andy. "The Wilderness: Where we learn the lessons of faith." Secrets from Ancient Paths. YouTube. May 27, 2022. https://www.youtube.com/watch?v=7LR27illW7A

IMMANUEL

Evans, Tony. *The Power of Jesus' Names*. Harvest House: Eugene, OR. 2019.

Sherwood, Ben. *The Survivors' Club*. Grand Central Publishing: New York. 2009.

WONDERFUL

Wiersbe, Warren. *The Names of Jesus*. 10Publishing: England. 1997.

Travis, Suzi, "Has the Internet Changed the Landscape of Human Curiosity?" Medium.com. September 12, 2023.

COUNSELOR

Leeby, Cheralyn. "The Psychology of the Modern Day Social Media Influencer." *Psychology Today*. January 2, 2024. https://www.psychologytoday.com/us/blog/consciously-creating-your-soul-life/202401/the-psychology-of-the-modern-day-social-media

PRINCE OF PEACE

"I Heard the Bells on Christmas Day." https://en.wikipedia.org/wiki/I_Heard_the_Bells_on_Christmas_Day

Simpson, A.B. *The Names of Jesus*. CreateSpace Independent Publishing Platform, March 2014.

LORD

Hawn, C. Michael. "History of Hymns: Away in a Manger." UMCdiscipleship.com. June 2013.

https://www.umcdiscipleship.org/resources/history-of-hymns-away-in-a-manger

BREAD OF LIFE

Vedder, Lee. "Stollen: This German Bread is a Holiday Highlight." December 16, 2019. https://blog.bakewithzing.com/stollen-german-christmas-bread

Ross, Katelyn and Samuels, Jon. "Georgia man tackles student lunch debt with savory treat." 11alive Exclusives. August 12, 2024. https://www.11alive.com/article/news/special-reports/11alive-exclusives/cleveland-white-county-georgia-peanut-stand

THE WORD

Boes, Chelsea, "The Portal in Their Pockets," WORLD radio. 3.27.2024. https://wng.org/podcasts/the-portal-in-their-pockets-1711473861

THE GREAT PHYSICIAN

"Jesus the Great Physician," Ligonier Ministries. February 2, 2016. https://www.ligonier.org/learn/devotionals/jesus-great-physician

Balconi M, Sansone M, Angioletti L. "Consumers in the Face of COVID-19-Related Advertising: Threat or Boost Effect?" *Front Psychol*. 2022 Mar 7;13:834426. doi: 10.3389/fpsyg.2022.834426. PMID: 35345640; PMCID: PMC8957070.

Wilkin, Jen. *None Like Him*. Crossway: Wheaton, IL. 2016.

RABBI

"Meet Michelle Gowan." CanvasRebel, March 4, 2024. https://canvasrebel.com/meet-michelle-gowan/

LORD OF HOSTS

"What is Trooping the Color?" https://www.royal.uk/what-is-trooping-the-colour

SON OF GOD, SON OF MAN

Evans, Tony. *The Power of Jesus' Names*. Harvest House: Eugene, OR. 2019.

THE WAY

Olson, Bruce. *Bruchko*. Charisma House: Lake Mary, FL. 2006

THE TRUTH

Childers, Alisa. *Live Your Truth and Other Lies.* Tyndale Momentum: Carol Stream, IL. 2022

REDEEMER

Crawford, Les. "Jesus, Our Kinsman Redeemer." The Friends of Israel Gospel Ministry, February 2, 2024. https://www.foi.org/2024/02/02/jesus-our-kinsman-redeemer/

SOON COMING KING

Poblete, Alyssa. "Joy to the World: A Christmas Hymn Reconsidered." The Gospel Coalition. December 22, 2014. https://www.thegospelcoalition.org/article/joy-to-the-world-a-classic-christmas-hymn-reconsidered/

LAMB OF GOD

"Best Church Nativity Pageant Ever: Sheep Steals Baby Jesus, Mary Saves Him." *Today.* December 13, 2017. https://www.today.com/parents/best-church-nativity-pageant-ever-sheep-steals-baby-jesus

Evans, Tony. *The Power of Jesus' Names*. Harvest House: Eugene, OR. 2019.

BRIDEGROOM

Piper, John. "Jesus Christ, The Bridegroom, Past and Future." Desiring God. April 4, 2004. https://www.desiringgod.org/messages/jesus-christ-the-bridegroom-past-and-future

ABOUT THE AUTHOR

Chrissie Smith is a Bible teacher, speaker, and author. She is also employed as a contracting officer for the Department of Defense.

She is the author of eight books (Available on Amazon):

- *Advent to Advent*
- *The Wondrous Gift*
- *Glory: Rescued, Redeemed, Transformed*
- *Journey of Hope*
- *Not Fit to Eat: Dishes and Thoughts from a Vintage Southern Kitchen.*
- *Adorned for Eternity*
- *Where He Dwells*
- *Soul Anchors (*Only available from the author. Seriously—don't buy this one from Amazon).

She resides in Perry, Georgia. You can contact her at chrissieosmith@gmail.com.

Made in the USA
Columbia, SC
19 November 2024

46633311R00080